To Maddison, without your notes and provocation,
this book would have been written in half the time...
and be half as good! I love you.

Contents

Winning the Room

Public speaking skills for *unforgettable* storytelling.

Jonathan Pease

mango
PUBLISHING

CORAL GABLES

Cover Design: Lila Theodoros
Cover Photo/illustration: Lila Theodoros
Layout & Design: Lila Theodoros + Elina Diaz
Researcher and go-to sounding board: Cathie McGinn

For permission requests, please contact the publisher at:
Mango Publishing Group
2850 S Douglas Road, 2nd Floor
Coral Gables, FL 33134 USA
info@mango.bz

For special orders, quantity sales, course adoptions and corporate sales, please email the publisher at sales@mango.bz. For trade and wholesale sales, please contact Ingram Publisher Services at customer.service@ingramcontent.com or +1.800.509.4887.

Winning the Room: Public Speaking Skills for Unforgettable Storytelling

Library of Congress Cataloging-in-Publication number: 2023930437
ISBN: (paperback) 978-1-68481-122-9, (hardcover) 978-1-68481-286-8, (ebook) 978-1-68481-123-6
BISAC category code: LAN026000, LANGUAGE ARTS & DISCIPLINES / Public Speaking & Speech Writing

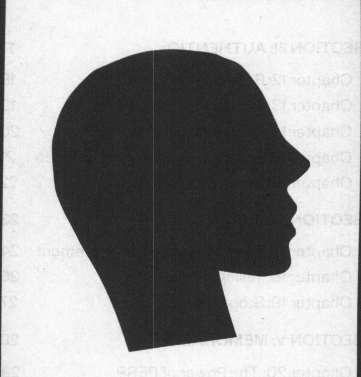

Preface

Being an excellent public speaker is often thought of, or even dismissed, as a talent people either have or don't have. And as a person writing a book on the topic, you may think I must be one of the blessed few.

I want to make my position clear: the ability to public speak in an engaging way that connects with your audience as intended is a skill that anyone can develop and master.

I know this is true first-hand because I avoided public speaking for almost half my life until I made it my mission to figure it out. Like most people who figure something out and create a method, this came from a place of pain.

If you question whether you will ever overcome your challenges in this space, I hope that by sharing my early predicaments and fears, you will resonate with my journey and have some more confidence as you read on. To take it a step further—and on a more positive and less fear-based note—I also want you to read on feeling inspired by how transformational excellent public speaking can be.

As a child, I had a lot of learning and behavioural issues. If I were a young person today, I would probably be considered neurodivergent, but I was just classified as "difficult" back then. I struggled with focus and basic concepts, and I have never spoken about this before, but I also silently struggled with a stutter.

There are a few different types of stutters or "disfluency." For me, it presented as mental blocks on words. I would be mid-sentence, everything feeling normal, and then one word would get caught in my throat or mind—or both. I couldn't get the word to come out.

This mental block quickly became physical, and as I tried to force the term to come out, the physiological response would leave me looking as though I was having a spasm. I was hugely embarrassed by these moments; they made me feel dumb and inferior. I dreaded them happening, making the moments worse and more regular.

These days, I can recognise someone with a stutter a mile off before I even hear them get stuck on a word. When I see others displaying this kind of behaviour, I cringe and get feelings of anxiety and embarrassment. Weirdly, I was social and chatty in everyday life. My parents and teachers always said I had the "gift of the gab." The problem was that the words would stop flowing as soon as I felt any pressure. I'd get stuck on specific terms and often end up in deafening silence. That would result in the people around me noticing, staring (or at least it felt that way), and me burning with more embarrassment.

Like any difficulty holding you back, you learn to create workarounds or find ways to mask it. So, I avoided any moments where I might have to speak in public (and for someone who loved to be the centre of attention, this was acutely painful). Or, failing that, resort to things like faking a cough or physical pain (like rubbing my "sore" hand). I became a master of misdirection; I would try almost anything to take the attention away from me in those moments.

But either way, I would still get furious at myself. I am a highly competitive person, so the idea of sabotaging myself was annoying. It's like kicking an own goal.

It wasn't until my early twenties that I realised I could no longer work around these limitations. Instead, I needed to train myself to get over them and thrive.

Fast forward to my first corporate job.

I was working in the advertising industry in New York, where everyone is meant to be a fabulous storyteller. In my experience, Americans are born orators! I was too embarrassed even to hint I didn't have this skill, let alone admit I still panicked at the thought of it.

I would usually call in sick if I had to present to a client or even in an internal meeting. If that weren't an option, I'd manoeuvre the situation to ensure others would present. I was junior enough that it didn't materially matter; I wouldn't be that missed. Someone else would always pick up the slack and present on my behalf. But I was indeed missing opportunities.

I had a niggling voice telling me I needed to stop being like this. But I needed more time to solve this issue. Maybe next week. Maybe next year.

Like a mirror to my delinquency in this area, my boss at the time was a natural, always pitching with ease and excellence. But for me, sleepless nights, significant anxiety, public humiliation, and too many forced sick days were my ongoing reality. I couldn't get past the question, "What is wrong with me and right with him?" It felt like a glitch in the matrix.

I was never aware of his special training, but as good as he was, he was still obsessed with mastering the craft of presenting rather than relying on natural abilities or winging it. His relentless rehearsals pre-pitch and brutal feedback sessions post-pitch were legendary. My observations and endless notes about how he consistently shot the lights out with ease and grace were the first seeds that grew into this book.

* * *

The second catalyst also came from my time in New York at this job. I already knew from my direct boss that great pitching could sell ideas to clients and that I needed to get better at it to avoid career limitations and personal embarrassment. Still, I hadn't yet realised the broader power it could have on human behaviour and success.

This lesson came after I heard the abrupt news that my ultimate boss and mentor at BBDO New York, Phil Dusenbery, was leaving the business. I still remember the all-staff email in March 2002 like it was yesterday. I can't communicate how much he meant to me and what a big deal his departure was.

Phil was irreplaceable to me. Along with fashion designer Diane von Furstenberg, he dragged me into the industry. He believed in me and gave me my shot. He even gifted me his high-powered immigration lawyer to help secure a working visa, which in those days was incredibly hard to come by.

We were called to an uptown venue on the day of Phil's departure to hear from Phil but mainly to meet his replacement, who was flying in from London for the occasion.

As I walked up 6th Avenue on that cold, crisp morning with a bunch of my colleagues, I recall all of us being distinctly sombre. Many people in the company shared my sentiment about this transitional moment for the agency. We were not feeling receptive to the guy stepping in. He was about to address a tough crowd.

Like good corporate citizens, we turned up and shuffled

into the large auditorium. There were over 1,500 people jammed in, and it was standing-room only. We all milled around waiting, muttering grumpily, until eventually, the room fell quiet. Phil said a few humble and, as always, enlightened words and then stepped back to welcome his replacement to the stage.

He spoke to us for at most eight minutes. In that short time, he converted everyone. From a doubter to a believer, from an adversary to a loyal teammate. In eight minutes! It blew me away. I couldn't fathom the power of one great speech. It was transformational. He had us all joining him as allies on this new journey for him and BBDO.

It was right there, at that moment, that I realised I was on a burning platform. I had to fix this *now* and make public speaking a part of my life. I needed to overcome this self-imposed limitation where I'd told myself that I couldn't public speak and didn't need to public speak to get ahead in life.

I would become someone who could turn up and present effectively.

I immediately threw myself at the problem and madly researched the world's best courses (and best presenters). I was flush with great options. Over the next few years, I attended courses in New York, LA, Toronto, London, and Sydney. I even expanded to vocal classes, opera singing classes, acting coaching, NLP training, and the communications course at the Church of Scientology...that was an eye-opener!

Whilst I learned much theory and got a broader understanding of the subject matter, I needed tangible things to put into practice. Feeling underwhelmed, I collected what I liked from all those courses and started my curation journey.

I watched hours and hours of public speakers I loved. Some were my original bosses at BBDO, from Grammy winners to cult gurus, business mavericks, charismatic street performers, and iconic world leaders. I wrote down all the practical tips I could find, observe, and extract.

I then started practising them myself. By this stage in my career, I was pitching to clients semi-regularly, and it was a fantastic testing ground.

At first, I practised with my colleagues, and as I became more senior, I trained my teams with the tools I was gathering. I eventually started working with clients, organisations, and leaders in the public eye.

All types of people from all walks of life.

These learnings evolved into what has today become my *Winning the Room* course and methodology.

I no longer work purely in advertising, and I'm not a full-time public speaking coach. Chief Creative Officer is my day job, and I love so many aspects of that gig. I also love making films, investing in start-ups, and many other passions.

But the thing I love the most is pitching. I get my absolute satisfaction—my juice—from those precious moments in the room, presenting my guts out!

It's still hard to believe something that started as a deficit has become my obsession.

So, if you're currently working with a stutter, nerves, or any other difficulties, I feel you. It's a silent and slow nightmare. I want to give you hope that you can get over it. It came down to pausing, breath control, and the eventual confidence that grew and grew as I started to get the better of it.

It's a theme you'll be hearing more about in this book, but I can't stress it enough: practice, practice, and more practice. To this day, I consciously find ways to decrease the pressure and use a few strategies to manage it. I'll explain the main techniques that work for me in this book—and for the thousands of people I've coached.

You might think I'm labouring the point, but if I can go from someone who used to be on the verge of faking his death to get out of presenting to someone who pitches for a living, whose career hinges on their ability to win rooms... So. Can. You.

The more I learn about public speaking, the more I enjoy it. Like most things in life, the more you can enjoy something, the better you will get at it, and the better you get, the more you will enjoy it. It's a self-fulfilling prophecy.

I hope that after you've read this book, you take steps to find joy in presenting, too.

Introduction

Everyone, whether we realise it or not,
relies on public speaking daily.
In simple terms, when you talk to anyone
outside of the comfort of your head,
you're public speaking.

This book is designed for everyone. Not just keynote speakers, storytellers, and deal makers.

If you want to bring even one person along with you and your ideas, you need to learn the art and science of public speaking.

Before we roll into the content, though, let's quickly talk about the title of this book and method: *Winning the Room*.

The notion of "winning" can be a polarising term in our culture—at its worst, it implies a sense that one is selfish and uncollaborative. I believe that when we win in public speaking—and arguably in business or life—we can connect with others around an idea and create something new, powerful, and meaningful together.

Winning the Room in this context means achieving the objectives we set out to accomplish with what we are saying— for people to believe, invest, or follow you, whether at a new job interview, a speech at your best friend's wedding, or a pitch to investors.

In various areas of life, we all need to make our points, tell our engaging stories to the largest possible audience, and be remembered.

My belief—which has become more of a certainty with the experience I've gained—is that we need to engage with other people to achieve great things. If you have a brilliant idea, you can take it a long way alone, but to get to "great," we must learn to unlock the power of the collective. Getting other people to come on the journey with you is exhilarating. It's fun and gets you somewhere much more exciting than you could ever have travelled alone.

You'll notice I use the words *indelible* and *attention* often in this book. We live in the attention age, so we're all playing the attention game, whether we like it or not. It's a game where the people who get and hold attention win. Earning and maintaining attention, and then making your pitch indelible, is the act of putting an idea into the minds of your audience that's impossible to forget.

Through the techniques in this book, you'll be able to create a deep connection with the audience, which means that when they recall your interaction or idea, it's a positive memory. And when that happens, there are no losers. It's a win-win.

✳ ✳ ✳

Back to storytelling as a human trait.

Despite the involuntary wince most people have in reaction to these words, public speaking is your birthright as a human. Our species evolved through telling stories to one another. Centuries ago, we gathered around the fire, sharing experiences and making myths, and these days we watch tiny digital screens with the same intention: to feel a connection and a sense of belonging.

You don't need to be an expert in evolutionary psychology to excel in public speaking, but let's start by accepting that our abilities to tell stories, and to connect around ideas, have enabled humans to survive and thrive over millennia.

Storytelling and idea sharing were once skills everyone held in common, but somewhere along the way, many of us lost these talents or began to think of them as jobs other people did.

Your existence proves that your ancestors were great at working collectively using the power of ideas. From bartering to banter, standing in front of another person and using words to persuade, engage, and even charm them is an essential part of what makes us human. And as technology, automation, and machine learning make inroads into more and more areas of our lives, being uniquely human will become ever more vital.

If public speaking is something you struggle to do, it's not that you've somehow evolved away from this capability: it's only that you've lost the belief that you can do it. Remind yourself: You are as capable of sharing your ideas as any other individual on this planet. All you need are proven techniques and strategies to help you win any room you walk into, which this book aims to do for you.

In today's world, it's easier to let other people or things do the talking—send an email, a quick text or DM, or chat to a chatbot—and harder to be heard.

Far from communicating predominantly with the local village, these days, we are now inundated with information and ideas from all over the world—media, social media, politics, and advertising. Even on an individual level, everyone is a content hub, and we're consuming their stories across every platform.

There is noise everywhere, and it's overwhelming just thinking about it.

Consider this: while we go about our days being targeted with all these messages, forcing our brains to filter out 99 percent of the noise, *our* success in work and life relies on others taking notice of *our* messages.

Therefore, the difference between success and failure comes down to figuring out: How does your story become part of the 1 percent of noises others hear and act on?

When you break it down, the goal of any storytelling or public speaking moment is to cut through the noise and capture your audience's increasingly short attention spans so they engage with and buy into your message. This is the fundamental premise behind *Winning the Room*.

Even if you have a solid and vital message, whether you achieve this goal (in other words, if anyone cares about it or not) ultimately comes down to how you are in the way you speak with your audience. Can you forge a genuine connection and bring them on the journey with you?

The concepts of "cut-through" and "authenticity" are the cringeworthy marketing buzzwords *du jour*. Still, I'm ready to defend them—especially authenticity, at least in its purest form—as *the* holy grail of public speaking.

That said, I think merely striving to "cut through" and "be authentic" oversimplifies the task at hand and lands us in the space of ripe-for-mocking self-help gurus on social media. I'm striving for practicality here.

Everything we're about to go through is immediately actionable. That's my number one priority in this book. My number two priority is to ensure that everything has been road-tested. All the ideas and tips in this book have been used by me, my teams, and my clients.

Nothing is in here because it sounds smart or is theoretically good, or I've read it in a book by someone I respect. I have combed through a mountain of material and tried out a bunch of techniques, and only the best of the best made it into this book.

I see myself as a curator who has pulled together the absolute best public speaking tips, techniques, and fundamentals. I've thoroughly road-tested them, as have my teams and coaching clients. I've been pitching an idea a day (roughly speaking) for twenty years. I haven't bothered doing the math, but it's a lot of pitching. During that time, I've slowly figured out what works and what doesn't.

I get so much joy from seeing the people I work with change and improve. I've facilitated hundreds of *Winning the Room* workshops with thousands of participants and witnessed remarkable transformations over the years.

Most people I work with already have great ideas, but they often fall short when bringing others along for the ride with them. I've seen people go from not believing they had much to offer to becoming creative leaders, business leaders, and community leaders purely based on the way they learned to communicate their ideas.

People don't just gain a new skill set. More than that, they access a whole new dimension in both their working and personal lives.

✳ ✳ ✳

I've written this book to make this material easy to grasp and use. As part of that process, I created a methodology called **CLAIM**, which stands for **C**onfident, **L**ikeable, **A**uthentic, **I**nfluential, and **M**emorable. Your audience must believe you have these five attributes if you want you and your ideas to be persuasive and unforgettable. Moreover, you need to believe you have these attributes, too!

The content itself is not genius, and the book shouldn't be a challenging read. When broken down, the genius is that it's brilliantly simple.

What you're about to read in this book works. None of this stuff is purely theoretical. It's actionable. It's road-tested. It's meant for everyone. It's easy to grasp.

And most importantly, it'll make a difference in your life. And I want to be clear: though I reference advertising a lot due to my background, I'm not only talking about advertising pitches. These techniques can help you win any room, however large or small.

I fully understand that most people reading this book will be short on time. We all are these days. As a result, I've attempted to write this book with three modalities in mind.

Modality one is for the seriously time-poor. I invite you to read the section introductions (there are five of them) and the first piece in each chapter. It's the first paragraph or two above the section break in each chapter. This reading exercise will take you no more than one hour in total. I believe this alone will make you think differently about public speaking and at least bring your awareness to the things you could work on in the future to lift your game. You don't know what you don't know.

Modality two is for people who want to invest more time from the get-go or maybe after you've done Modality One and are now ready to dive deeper. For you, the instructions are straightforward: Read the book cover to cover, as you have time, and find opportunities in your everyday personal and professional worlds to apply what you learn and keep building on your skills. This experience is as close to doing a Winning the Room workshop with me IRL as I could put on paper. I know from hundreds of workshops that this will elevate your public speaking performance and give you an edge in work and life.

Modality three is for people who want to come on the journey and transform how they communicate in public. For you, my favourite type of people, complete modality two, ideally within a short period so you can best connect and consolidate the learnings, and then join the Winning the Room community at winningtherooms.com. It's a place where I continue to develop core and specialised courses and work with the group to improve their skills and prepare for specific presentations.

Public speaking is my obsession, and I get joy from working with people on their presentations. Becoming great at pitching requires many skills, rehearsing, and above all—time. And the best way for me to support you on that journey is through an ongoing relationship. A situation where we can share learnings for months if not years.

Working alone, we often lack the discipline to push ourselves. Pitching alone, you never get to rehearse properly or receive honest feedback. Whether you want to structure more memorable pitch stories, grow your confidence, influence your audience, or all of the above—the Winning the Room community provides the accountability and push you need to achieve your potential and win more pitches.

I'm not a futurist, but I am inspired by what is coming next. As technology makes inroads into more and more areas of our lives, being uniquely human and able to connect with other humans is becoming ever more vital.

Just getting the information out is not enough. Computers can already do that faster and better than you. The only X Factor you have left is the ability to make it emotive and honest and, in the process, make a real connection.

Public speaking is fundamentally about human connection, so public speaking skills will only get more valuable. As we automate and robotise everything, your ability to tell your story and pitch live in the moment will be crucial to your success.

Being a great public speaker should be your top priority for your ongoing relevance and maybe even your continuing employment and enjoyment in life.

Considering you bought this book, you may already agree.

In Memoriam

Phil Dusenberry was an industry giant who gave me more of his precious time than I deserved. Phil passed away just after Christmas in 2007. I'll always be hugely grateful for his mentorship, creative guidance, and support.

Confident

SECTION I

Hold it too tight, and you'll crush it.
Hold it too loose, and it'll fly away.

I start with confident because, while all the content in this book is interrelated, confidence is the bedrock and underpins everything else. All the tips, techniques, and other elements either contribute to or are enhanced by confidence...or, conversely, are completely undermined and let down by a lack of it.

Confidence in the context of public speaking is two-fold. There's the internal element of how you feel as the presenter, which is probably what you're used to focusing on when you think of confidence. Then there is the external element: how the audience perceives you. Regardless of how you feel, do they think you are confident and therefore to be believed and followed?

Confidence is an unusual thing. When you've got it, you can't understand why other people don't have it. And when you don't have it, it's hard to imagine how you'll ever get any. The content in this section will help you cultivate confidence internally, as well as help you do things that will express confidence externally. There's a nice positive loop here, too, because feeling confident will help you seem confident, and acting confident will help you feel more confident.

Confidence is critical because, in the public speaking game, your audience is more likely to pay attention to you and believe your message when you're confident and perceived as confident. They'll probably believe you if you're confident, and if you're not, they probably won't. It's that simple.

Try to think of a great public speaker, thought leader, or community elder who doesn't project confidence when they present. I bet you can't. It makes sense—why would anyone want to follow you if you're not confident about where you're going?

From an individual perspective, we were born confident. All of us were once supremely, unshakeably confident. When our chubby toddler fists reached for an object or when we demanded attention, it never entered our minds to wonder if we would be listened to or understood. We may never be able to return to that state of pure ego—and that's probably an excellent thing—but we can use the tips and techniques I've tested over the years and gathered in this book to make what was once our first nature become second nature.

Confidence can feel precarious because it can be unravelled so quickly. Nothing undermines confidence like someone telling you to "just be more confident." Hold it too tightly and you can crush it; too loosely and it slips through your fingers.

Relying on tangible tips rather than winging it with a vibe is like an insurance policy for maintaining confidence in the best and worst times.

Most star performers, sports people, and public speakers will admit they have a sneaking fear that one day they'll choke: get the yips,[1] freeze, or lose their mojo when they need it most. We often think of confidence in almost supernatural terms; it's why performers often have rituals or superstitions to ward off an attack of performance anxiety.

Many celebrities have quirky pre-show routines, from Tony Robbins's power posing and screaming sequence to

---

1 Philip Clarke, David Sheffield, Sally Akehurst. "Personality Predictors of Yips and Choking Susceptibility." *Frontiers in Psychology*. Jan 2020. pubmed.ncbi.nlm.nih.gov/32038345.

Rihanna, who famously has a shot of liquor before a gig to help overcome her stage fright.

The scrutiny and expectations surrounding a performer at the top of their game are incredibly daunting. But you don't need to aim for that kind of perfection. I'll discuss keeping things a little loose later in this book. You need to be self-possessed enough to know that you can stand up in front of your chosen audience and give it your best shot without fearing falling flat on your face.

It's another reason "faking it 'til you make it" won't cut it. Without a solid foundation of confidence, even if you manage to wing it for a while, one of these days, you'll hit a bump in the road; something will throw you off, and you'll find yourself having that deer-in-the-headlights moment that is so painful to witness—and worse to experience. There are simple techniques and skills to help you build and practice confidence, making it feel more predictable, achievable, and less fragile.

The kind of confidence that wins the room and inspires people to invest in your ideas can't be artificial. It needs to be authentic and grounded in genuine self-belief. An internal conviction results in outward confidence.

The first person you need to convince is yourself.

Feeling confident will free you up to engage with your listener. And when your audience thinks you ooze confidence, they will position you as a subject-matter expert. People want to engage with and buy from confident people.

Your audience is smart enough to know when someone is faking it. We might be sophisticated urban dwellers with supercomputers in our back pockets, but we're also still mammals who are highly attuned to each other's body language. We can spot "tells" or microexpressions, those momentary involuntary facial muscle twitches or tics that reveal how someone feels—whether we are consciously aware of this or not—and the impact on our perception is immediate and hard to shift.

Research indicates that not only can we smell fear, but it can also be contagious. A growing body of evidence shows that *chemosignals*[2] (which you know better as body odour)—especially those containing "threat-based information," like anxiety, disgust, or aggression—can transmit these feelings to the person detecting the scent.

Not only does this sound like a distinctly unpleasant meeting environment, but people experiencing your anxiety or detecting a whiff of doubt and fear, even second-hand, are unlikely to be receptive or open to your pitch because there's a good chance they are catching your vibe and becoming uncomfortable.

Trying to bluster or blag your audience is risky, with a high likelihood of failure. It also won't feel good to you, making it more likely that your negative feelings about public speaking will become more entrenched.

To think about it differently: Why would you want to white-knuckle it when you can cruise? And why would you want to pitch an idea you don't believe in? Do you genuinely want to spend your life delivering something you don't think is worth doing?

---

2 Jasper H.B. de Groot, Monique A.M. Smeets, Annemarie Kaldewaij, Maarten J.A. Duijndam, Gün R Semin. 2012. "Chemosignals Communicate Human Emotions." *Psychological Science*. 23:1417–1424. 2012.

Being confident and having the skills to cultivate confidence will help your delivery and overall performance—and perhaps it's what gets you to agree to speak in the first place.

As you might imagine, confidence begets confidence. The more confident you are, the more confident you become. The more you practice these skills, the more natural they will become and the more authentic your confidence will become. Unfortunately, the reverse is also true, so the more you lose confidence, the less confident you will become. It's a slippery slope. The life lesson here is to do the prep work now to ensure you set yourself up for the success track, not more misery.

Again, we focus first on confidence because confident public speakers feel believable. They are easy to trust, and they feel like they're experts in their content. If you want to be remembered, you will have to get confident.

Before we dive too far into the breakdown of how to present with confidence, though, I'd like to make a few small but important distinctions.

Firstly, let's not confuse confidence with being loud or extroverted. This section, and this entire book, is not about making you become a louder, "jazz hands" kind of presenter. I regularly come across great public speakers who are soft-spoken. But they are still confident. The difference is they're quietly confident!

Secondly, there's a fine line between confidence and arrogance. Be sure of what you are saying, but don't forget to retain some humility. As a public speaker, you never want to come across as arrogant. It's an audience killer, and you will lose your audience's empathy for you almost immediately.

This section is about staying on the right side of that line. Confidence that engages and makes people believe. Confidence that is intelligent and authentic.

Thirdly, confidence isn't just about how you feel. It's also about how your audience perceives you. Do they think you are confident? It's one thing to be inwardly confident, but if you can't, or don't, communicate that confidence to your audience, you're not winning in anyone else's mind.

If you can strategically demonstrate that confidence to your audience, they will be more likely to give you their attention, engage with you, and at the end of the day, believe you.

I want to show you that there are ways of bolstering your inner confidence, but you also need to be conscious of how you project it. Our relationship to confidence must be an adjective and a verb: a practice.

We need to *be* confident but also "do" confidence.

This section explores five techniques that will help you build confidence internally and, even more importantly, help you demonstrate that confidence to your audience.

Chapter 1

OWN YOUR VOICE

"I'm tough, I'm ambitious,
and I know exactly what I want.
If that makes me a bitch, okay."

—Madonna Ciccone

I can't emphasise enough how important it is to find and use your voice to communicate effectively. The power of voice modulation in public speaking can significantly influence your audience's perception and improve understanding. This chapter will help you find your most natural and compelling speaking voice, help you understand the basics of how to modify tone and pitch and teach you some techniques to use as the cornerstone of your presentation process.

We all have a range of ways of communicating in different contexts. Still, you need to find your most authentic voice and practice using that one true voice to master speaking with confidence. Find your voice and own it.

We'll look at the physiology of the voice and how to use that to your advantage when you're projecting in the room, as well as some techniques to get you to own your true voice:

1. Hearing Your Real Voice
2. Using Your Breath
3. Find Your Voice
4. Shift Your Tone
5. Shift Your Pitch
6. Track and Practice

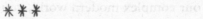

Most people I come across in my Winning the Room workshops don't think that much about their voices. Sure, they know they need their voice to get the words into the room, but they usually don't take full advantage of its range and what it can bring to any point and presentation.

Your voice is the most effective way of showing your audience who you are. It's your aural ID.

When I talk about finding your voice, I mean this in two ways. Firstly, finding the most authentic and unique way you communicate and honing that for maximum impact.

And secondly, locating your voice in your body and using some techniques to give that voice the fullest range of expression you're capable of, like a virtuoso playing an instrument.

Your voice is as personal, irreplaceable, and expressive as your face. And your audience, whether you're pitching in a boardroom or asking someone to go on a date with you, will be making judgments about who you are and what you stand for the second you open your mouth (or even before that). From your accent to timbre and use of slang, your voice gives other people a huge number of clues about who you are, and the unconscious biases of your audience will start to play out from the first word.

We can't alter these biases, but we can communicate with our audience from a position of such strength and confidence that we can direct their attention to our words—as well as how we say them.

Finding and using your most authentic voice is vital. In our complex modern world, you move in and out of vastly different social groups with whom you communicate in ways that may change substantially depending on context.

Adapting our language, vocal mannerisms, and even accent to be closer to that of the people we're talking to is an evolutionary skill we have developed; it's a shorthand to show we belong to the group.

Social scientists call this "code-switching," and it's another of those ways in which humans are incredibly creative and adaptable. Driven by a desire to fit in and be seen as acceptable—"one of us"—by the dominant culture or group in a particular situation, people can modify their language, use of the vernacular, and even their posture, to blend in.

It's clever and creative, but it comes at a cost. It can take a lot of effort to move between worlds, particularly if we're members of marginalised communities or the distance between how we communicate at home and work is expansive. This is even more pronounced if English isn't your first language or you're from a community that experiences discrimination—where code-switching comes from: the experience of people of colour, queer people, and women, navigating predominantly white, straight, male environments, which is often typical of the business world.

Even if you can quickly move fluidly between worlds, using your most authentic voice when public speaking is essential. Maintaining a voice that is distanced from our "true" voice places extra strain on our brains when all our available cognitive capacity should be focused on winning the room. Think of it like wearing a shoe with a stone in it. You can deal with it, and most of the time, you're not consciously aware of it, but it's always at the back of your mind, distracting you, and by the end of the day, you're on the way to having a blister.

To get deeper into these ideas, think about how people adapt their communication to fit into, or stand out from, their social context.

Research shows that when we try too hard to fit into modes of communication that might suit others, we can also lose connection to our "true" voice and risk seeming fake or bland.

Another word of warning: Because the way we communicate means navigating the complex power differentials at play in many work situations, trying to adapt to what we perceive as the style of our audience means we risk coming across as patronising or even discriminatory. If you're talking to more than one person, adapting your tone to match that of the bigwig means you can lose the rest of the room, and you might seem like an arse kisser, as we say in Australia.

And it's important to remember that our goal isn't to be homogeneous. We want to establish from the outset that we have a fresh, exciting perspective, and trying to blend in means losing our edge.

When I say your true voice, I mean the voice you use when you're at your most comfortable. It could be how you talk when you're at your mum's kitchen table or with your dearest friends, your phone voice, or the voice you use to give yourself a stern talking-to in the bathroom mirror.

Over the past couple of years, while we've all been stuck at home, I know several people who learned to their horror, that their significant other has a "work voice" they'd never heard before—and that it revealed some previously unknown aspect of their character that, as lockdown dragged on, they discovered they couldn't stand.

Another reason to be your authentic self wherever you go.

When we hear an engaging public speaker who can grab and hold our attention—it's often because of how they speak. Modulating your voice is critical.

In 1967, Professor Albert Mehrabian proposed the "7 percent–38 percent–55 percent rule" of human communication, in which he claimed that 90 percent of communication was nonverbal. You'll see that statistic floating around the internet even now. Although the data in this rule has been solidly disproven, most researchers agree that the actual words contained in our communication have a significantly less overall impact than body language, facial expressions, gestures, and tone.

We'll dive more deeply into body language in Chapters 12 and 17.

This isn't to say your content doesn't matter. But let's assume that everyone who gets a meeting with your potential investor, client, or new boss will have something good to offer, maybe as good as your content—maybe better. That part is just the price of admission.

How you deliver this content will make the most significant difference. Think of your content as a Formula One car and your voice as the driver. Everyone knows the car is hugely impressive, but it's all about the driver.

The way the driver moves and performs showcases the car's power. You never get off the starting grid without using your voice to animate the content.

Think of how a virtuoso musician can extract an incredible array of sounds from a single instrument.

Skilled public speakers work in the same way; they alter their pitch, tone, resonance, and volume depending on the message they are trying to communicate. Like learning an instrument, modulating your voice takes time and practice, but it is a skill worth learning and an essential part of being an accomplished public speaker.

Excellent voice modulation is like a catchy piece of

music that stays with you. It's got structure. An introduction, a tempo, moments that build up energy and moments that calm down energy, and finally, the crescendo. There's a rhythmic story that happens in a strong presentation, something melodic and compelling to how the speaker uses their voice beyond the words themselves to grab attention and create a powerful impact on their audience.

Like everything in this book, you need to think about what is authentic to you and what makes sense for your style. I'm not recommending you become high-energy and loud if that isn't natural. But no matter how quiet and reserved you think you are, everyone has a range to play with. It's not about becoming someone else; it's about accentuating what you have.

A cautionary tale for people who think they need to be serious to be taken seriously and therefore don't want to move their voice around too much: I regularly work with C-suite clients who deal with facts and figures that they need to communicate to the market on behalf of their organisation. They are in the business of being accurate, but the great ones also know that they need to inspire with confidence. Try listening to a board update with no voice modulation. It's the definition of a boring room.

A great presenter can add colour and story to even the straightest facts and figures without adding artificial drama— just by modulating their voice.

A tone of voice that is inconsistent with your words affects your credibility. If you're talking about an exciting idea in a flat voice,[3] the contrast between your voice and your content can create a fundamental disconnect for the audience. If your words and your tone aren't consistent, there is evidence that audiences will see you as less believable.[4]

It's like trying to depict a rainbow using grey paint.

For every point you make in your presentation, there's a way you can use your voice to make that point more clearly and powerfully. It sounds obvious: A voice that moves around a lot and accentuates points with changes in tone will hold more attention and be more interesting. Why wouldn't everybody speak like that in public? Well, the answer is simple and comes back to confidence. As soon as you're in that public speaking spotlight, nerves come in. You're looking around the audience; you start to get concerned about whether you know your material, maybe catch a glimpse of someone you know, and you start feeling self-conscious... All these things happen in an instant.

When all of this happens, most people grab onto the only thing that seems certain in that room: their content. They start ploughing straight through the middle of it in a monotone voice, getting from slide one to the end. And you lose your listeners along the way. Your audience isn't deliberately being rude or inattentive; you're unintentionally giving them permission to disregard your words.

If we think about this from a neuroscience perspective, the human brain is hard-wired to pay more attention to

3 Randall L. Gillis, Elizabeth S. Nilsen. "Consistency between Verbal and Non-Verbal Affective Cues: A Clue to Speaker Credibility." *Cognition & Emotion*. 2017. pubmed. ncbi.nlm.nih.gov/26892724.

4 "Consistency between Verbal and Non-Verbal Affective Cues: A Clue to Speaker Credibility."

negative stimuli than positive ones. It's one of those skills that kept us alive in prehistoric times (and now causes us so much stress). Conversely, when we've categorised something as not demanding much concentration, our brains are saving energy by going into sleep mode. It's why keeping our eyes open can genuinely feel impossible when someone is droning on in a meeting. In a nutshell, being monotonous—to be flat and monotone—makes it harder for people to pay attention to you, let alone to process how they feel about your big ideas.[5]

Sounds logical, but how the hell does anyone do it? Well, firstly, you need to figure out the pitch and range of your voice and whether you're even used to speaking in your most natural voice.

Hearing Your Real Voice

Starts with learning to love your voice. Many of us don't, and there's a simple reason for that: the voice you hear when you speak isn't the one arriving in other people's ears. You're used to hearing it through the conductivity of the bones and soft tissues in your head, not through resonance in the air. When you listen to a recording of yourself, your voice can sound higher-pitched, flatter, or less rounded than you're used to.

Try recording yourself speaking and listening back to yourself every day until you get used to it. And get over the idea that you need a "professional" voice—your audience will

---

5   "A speaker's tone of voice (speaking rate, tone of voice, and intonation), as well as acoustical cues to the identity of a speaker, routinely impacts the affective state of the listener." Lynne C. Nygaard, Jennifer S. Queen. "Communicating emotion: Linking affective prosody and word meaning." *Journal of Experimental Psychology: Human Perception and Performance.* 34:1017–1030 2008. pubmed.ncbi.nlm.nih. gov/18665742.

be just as engaged by a voice that moves and is interesting as they will by a perfect voice.

Using Your Breath

You might need to unlearn some habits, from breathing too shallowly to the use of rising inflection—where every sentence goes up at the end, so everything sounds like a question— which many younger people have adopted. Some of these tendencies can undermine the confidence and gravitas you need to win the room, but the good news is that they can all be overcome with practice.

Staying relaxed is key. Voice is amplified vibration, and any tension in your jaw, soft palate, lips, or shoulders will flatten your resonance and limit your vocal range.

Another useful hack is to yawn deeply as part of your warm-up—although I don't recommend you do this in front of your audience. As you yawn, think about stretching your soft palate and pushing the tip of your tongue to the back of your front teeth. Check your jaw and if you notice you're clenching your teeth, massage the muscles to release any tightness; it's another way of releasing tension and getting your voice ready to perform at its best.

You don't need to shout to be heard. Projecting your voice means using your diaphragm. Try taking a big breath in, bringing as much air as deeply into your lungs as you feel you can hold, and letting your belly expand as you inhale. Then force all that air out with a big "haaaaa" sound. Play around with that sound, aiming it at the back wall of a room—then try it in a larger room. Ask someone you trust to give you feedback—and I'll go into the importance of rehearsing later in this book.

Find Your Voice

To figure out where your voice naturally sits, when you're relaxed and not straining to sound any particular way, try this exercise. This will help you to physically feel where you naturally speak from and identify the tone and pitch that's your default voice. Take a long, slow, deep inhale and imagine your breath going all the way to your core. Without holding anything in, allow your breath to flow out in a steady exhale, and still without effort, try adding a sound to that exhale. Notice where that sound is located—your chest, diaphragm, throat? Does it sound like your usual voice in terms of depth, tone, and timbre?

Shift Your Tone

Our voices are created by vibrations in our breath as it moves through three areas: nasal, oral, and pharyngeal. Thinking of the voice like an instrument again, you can play around with moving your breath through these different areas, using your voice and your physiology to create different effects.

Try getting playful—think of your face as your personal kazoo and see what happens when you push more of the air pressure through your nose; now your mouth; now the base of your throat. What does it do to the sound? What feeling does it give your listener? How high can you go? How low?

Using your natural voice, record yourself doing your speech. Then listen to it with your eyes closed; just listen for what your voice does. Does your voice strike a tone and then hold the same tone throughout, or does it move around naturally as you make different points, and take different shapes as the presentation unfolds?

Shift Your Pitch

I'll talk more about the importance of using your breath and getting physical in Chapter 3, but there are some simple exercises you can do to get more in touch with how your voice works and how to modulate it, project it—and have fun with it.

If you're not convinced that the pitch of your voice makes any real difference, a study of almost eight hundred male CEOs in the US found those with deeper voices were wealthier and ran larger companies.[6]

I'm not suggesting you put on a false baritone, but even if your natural voice is up in the rafters, you can still alter the pitch of your voice within that range. Knowing that a deeper pitch suggests gravitas, seriousness, and a perception of greater intelligence to the audience, use that change of pitch consciously. A higher pitch communicates excitement, and energy—perhaps you can use that at the moment you want the audience to lean into your big idea.

You could take your voice up and make it feel bright and sprightly when you're communicating something that's positive and different. You could even take your voice down to a whisper when you want your points to feel important and precious. Like a secret, your audience needs to lean forward to hear.

---

6   William J. Mayew, Christopher A. Parsons, Mohan Venkatachalam. "Voice Pitch and the Labor Market Success of Male Chief Executive Officers." *Evolution and Human Behavior*. July 2013.

Track and Practice

Go back to your speech, think about the piece as a whole, and decide where your emphasis and shifts in pitch, pacing, and so on need to be. I mark up my speech notes with specific markers for voice changes. I like to underline and mark in bold—use whatever notation works for you. For example, I will have a section that is bold and underlined. I know I'm going to make a big, positive, uplifting move with my voice. And then, maybe toward the end, the line will be underlined. And I know that at that point, I'm going to bring it down to a more meaningful moment, carrying more weight at the end of that sentence or section.

Finding your voice and then playing with the full range of expression you possess will help you bring your whole, most authentic self to your presentation. Rehearsing modulation like a maestro will solidify your confidence and help you connect with your listeners in a powerful way.

A voice that moves will move your audience more deeply.

Chapter 2

DEATH TO SMALL TALK

"I lose myself in music because
I can't be bothered explaining what I feel
to anyone else around me."

—Robert Smith

"Death to small talk" sounds like a sweeping statement, but I want to show you that, if anything, it's not strongly worded enough. In this chapter, I'm going to explain why small talk isn't your friend when you're public speaking, run through some of the potentially negative consequences of using small talk, and then talk about some techniques you can use instead.

I'll share some stories from my life that will make you seriously question ever uttering a skerrick of small talk again and run through three approaches I use.

The techniques we'll cover are:

1. Always Be Opening
2. Land the Intros
3. Drop It Like It's Hot

Small talk has its place, but I want to explain why that place is not in the room when you're presenting ideas.

Small talk makes us happy, research shows.[7] It's a great leveller, and it's a beneficial route to social connection and cohesion—and it is to be avoided at all costs. This might feel like an odd position to take within a section on confidence. Small talk makes people feel comfortable; feeling comfortable calms your nerves and puts you more at ease; being at ease arguably makes you feel more confident.

But our focus on confidence is not just about how you are feeling; it's about how your audience perceives you. And the latter matters more because if you're perceived as confident, then you'll feel more confident.

---

7 **Nicolas** Epley, Juliana Schroeder. "Mistakenly seeking solitude." *Journal of Experimental Psychology: General, 143*(5), 1980–1999.

This chapter focuses more on perception—how your audience perceives you before you've even started your speech (and therefore started to implement all the other tips and techniques in this chapter/book), and in the moments when you're not directly talking about the content of your pitch.

Small talk is a reflex action that many of us use to create a sense of safety and comfort. I want to show you that safety is the opposite of the energy you want to create in the room.

When we're pitching a big idea, we want to lean into the end of that spectrum that involves adventure, novelty, and excitement. Small talk is at the other end: it correlates with security and familiarity.

When you walk into the room, you need to have a sense of edge. Making the audience comfortable can take the shine off our status as outsiders, as an unknown quantity. You know the saying, "Familiarity breeds contempt"—well, I'm not suggesting your audience has contempt for you, but if you're pitching to extremely busy people who are making space in their diary for you, it's respectful to signal to them from the outset that you're here to give them something different and new and worth paying attention to. (And if you're not—why are you taking up their time and yours?)

Small talk belongs to the realm of the mundane—the uninspired, the familiar. We want to create a sense of magic. Have you ever seen a magician begin their act by chatting about their holiday plans or where to get the best coffee? Of course not. We're not in the room to manipulate our audience, but we aren't there to waste their time either. Eradicating small talk is one of the ways we demonstrate our respect for the people we're presenting to.

We want to take them on a journey, and why would they follow us if we're suggesting we're only going around the block, rather than somewhere new and exotic?

We want to grab and hold attention, not lull them into a misplaced sense of security.

When we're public speaking, we're creating a sensory impact on our audience. The way that this input, or stimulus, lands for our listener creates what's called an "affect."

On one end of the "affect" spectrum, we have high arousal or activation—that could range from excitement to fear. On the other end, we have low arousal, which we might experience as being sleepy, bored, or just disengaged. At the same time, the audience is interpreting the stimulus—our presentation—as pleasant or unpleasant.

In an ideal world, we'd like our audience to be in a state of high activation, and feeling a strong positive affect, but that's not a state we can maintain for long without constant new stimuli. And, as compelling as your content is, unless you're planning to tap-dance, make balloon animals, or break out into a Broadway show tune every few moments, you'll need to work hard to keep your audience switched on—and that begins when you start to speak.

You only have one opportunity to make your first impression, and walking into a room and dropping your energy so you can get comfortable means squandering that chance.

There is a weird zone, a liminal space, when you are first in the proximity of your audience but before you start your speech. It seems to warp time and energy levels, which work inversely with speakers and their audiences. They expect you to be warm, on peak form immediately, while in most cases you are coming in cold and warming up. Then, once they're getting tired, you're finally warmed up...and you're wasting greatness on people whose energy and activation levels are now dropping like a stone.

Not all small talk is equally sized.

Anthropologist Bronisław Malinowski, who I think it's fair to say would have been hard work at a dinner party, described it as "purposeless expressions of preference or aversions, accounts of irrelevant happenings...comments on what is perfectly obvious."[8]

The kind of chat Malinowski describes is what I want you to steer well clear of. There is a way to introduce what I call "strategic small talk": remarks which you've planned and rehearsed in advance and add value for your audience. They're on-topic, and they can work as chemistry-building content. This strategic small talk gives you a chance to start on the right foot and get straight to your content in a nice, welcoming, participatory way. Instead of "What are you up to this weekend?" start your presentation with a cool, interesting, attention-grabbing story.

I want to give you a real-life example of the pitfalls of starting small.

My team and I were presenting to a major FMCG (fast-moving consumer goods) client. We were doing an incredible job of making small talk: warm, charming, and engaging: asking about the client's kids and chatting about our weekend plans. And then in the midst of the small talk, we went off

8 Bronislaw Malinowski. "The Problem of Meaning in Primitive Languages." *Ogden & Richards.* pp. 296–336. 1923.

on a tangent all about the education system. Suddenly we were drawn into a deep conversation about the client's concerns with their kids' schooling and the areas the children were missing out on. On the surface, that was a moment of connection, which is what we all look for—it seemed fine—but we then got into our pitch, which was fundamentally about how we were going to sell more cereal for our multinational FMCG brand client. Try as we might, we could not stop the pitch from being pulled into the quicksand we had unwittingly waded into with our small talk. Instead of our well-rehearsed presentation, we found ourselves discussing whether cereal could offer a way to educate. What if we had educational elements in our idea and our marketing?

I'm not saying that there weren't lots of potentially great ideas in that mix—but it wasn't what we were there to pitch, and it became hugely distracting.

We couldn't get the client away from this line of thinking, and it muddled up our pitch. We ended up not being able to genuinely connect on the subject matter that we needed to get to a decision about.

In the end, what was memorable about that meeting was all the educational discussion we had up front. I'll talk more about ways you can take charge of the room and the conversation later in Chapter 15, but the key lesson here is that we inadvertently blundered into something that entirely side-tracked our audience and sent us down a cul-de-sac.

It can dilute your presentation and your points, and in the end, make you and your pitch anything but memorable.

Instead of buying into an idea that would have the customer going nuts for the product, the client went nuts over a conversational red herring.

I recall once we were presenting ideas to a regular client as part of our monthly "ideas retainer"—a rare and lucky arrangement to have in place in which we were paid to have ideas.

We took these monthly meetings seriously and as a result, we designed the hell out of them. On this occasion, one of the ideas we planned to present was an anti-technology product. This would be disruptive (and probably quite witty) considering the business was a technology-infused telco.

We walked into the room and started with our story. We had the whole room transfixed from word one, and in the end, they approved it and funded it on the spot. It was a big day for my fledgling agency.

What we didn't know was that the key decision-maker, whom we were close to, had lost a loved one earlier that week. Imagine we'd gone in with small talk…."How are you? What's been happening?" We would have undoubtedly gone down the path of hearing her terrible news. Pretty hard to bring the focus back to your ideas after that kind of introduction.

We found out about her situation the next day, and I checked in with her immediately. Surprisingly, she was so grateful that we'd jumped straight into our ideas. It was just the positive distraction she needed at that moment. This is an extreme example, but the lesson stays the same. If you waste time with small talk, you will undoubtedly drift off your plan and into distracting (and diluting) waters.

Okay, and now, with no preamble, let's cut straight to some practical tips.

Always Be Opening

You might know the conventional wisdom that when you're selling—an idea, a used car, whatever—that you must "always be closing." That phrase became mainstream in David Mamet's play (and subsequently the movie) *Glengarry Glen Ross*, where the desperate salespeople on the brink of burnout revealed the dark underbelly of the American dream and the cost of the "greed is good" ethos of the 1980s. The obsession with "closing"—getting a confirmed sale as fast as possible and pushing the prospect toward a yes whether they understand or benefit from the transaction—is probably one reason the notion of selling has some unsavoury associations today.

Rather than hustling someone toward a quick decision, I believe we should flip the dynamic to one of generosity and storytelling. Those first moments have a huge impact on the final outcome, and I'd argue a bigger, more intentional focus should be on the opener.

The first words you say in the room at the start of your presentation reach your audience at their fastest, most receptive, and paradoxically, most judgmental state of mind. Now that you know this, you must work with it and against your natural inclination to want to warm up slowly. One of the ways to do this is to make those powerful statements first—or at least lay some solid groundwork for building toward the "reveal" later. Think of this moment as the most precious one in your whole pitch, and don't waste it.

Land the Intros

Often, when we're presenting, there are new people in the room; people who don't know each other or who haven't met in person until this occasion. Ordinarily, introductions follow the same lacklustre formula. We've all witnessed it: person by person, we move around the table, and everyone gives a feeble "Hi, I'm so and so, and my role is whatever...."

Newsflash: this is one of the fastest ways to suck the energy out of any room. Land the Intros is a timely reminder that we need to make every aspect of our time in the room great, including the introductions, and make sure they're strategically interwoven into our presentation.

Firstly, choose someone on your team to introduce your whole team (if you're presenting alone, that choice will be easy). Secondly, figure out relevant stories about each person (or yourself) that relate directly to your presentation and the outcome you're looking to achieve. Maybe it's stories about that person's last job that position them as ideal experts for this type of project. Or maybe it's an outside-of-work passion or side hustle that makes them highly attuned to the target audience. Then, finally, deliver the introductions with passion and enthusiasm. Look people in the eyes, smile at your audience, and, importantly, smile at the people in your group as you introduce them. Done well, your introductions can be the running start you need to start winning.

Drop It Like It's Hot

Try to do what I call a hot intro. As soon as you get into the room, say a few hellos, but minimise this. Say little—and then start your pitch.

I can imagine this makes you feel uncomfortable—
and if you're feeling that way, it's working! If you feel
uncomfortable, imagine how your audience is feeling. When
we feel uncomfortable, we're paying attention.

Go straight into the pitch with no small talk at all. Now
that's powerful: that demonstrates that you are confident;
you're here for a reason; you respect your time, and you
respect the time of your audience. And you're not willing to
waste a minute. There's no better signal of the fact that you
mean business: you're here, it's important, and they need to
pay attention.

Because we're not here to fool around. We're here to
do something. We're here to pitch. It's powerful. And it will
change the way you pitch forever.

Experiment with this and find what works for you, but
this is one of those techniques that, once you do it, you may
realise it's a whole new way of pitching. Dare I say, it can be
a little addictive? Breezing straight through the conventions
and taking charge of the situation in a fresh, new way can feel
thrilling. Try it and let me know.

I'd love to give you an example of when I didn't use this
tip. I still wince a little when I think about it. It's what inspired
me to rethink how I used small talk and eventually led me to
the realisation that I needed to eradicate small talk altogether.

I was presenting to a large group of students in their
final year of high school. They were about to graduate. The
presentation took place in a big auditorium in Sydney, and I
had driven for hours to get there.

I knew there had been a big build-up in the morning,

and I felt the need to break the ice and lighten the load. I'd been alone in the car for four hours on the road there, with plenty of time to get relaxed, and I was ready to go. I knew exactly what I was going to do. I was Tight Loose—we'll talk about that later in this book.

When I got there, I found myself backstage, talking to some of the event organisers, and I fell into the small-talk trap. During that exchange, one of the people backstage told me that there were a lot of people in the audience from my old school, Geelong Grammar. If you're Australian, you probably know the school, but for the rest of the world, I should explain that Geelong Grammar is one of the most expensive, and arguably one of the best schools in Australia. If you were able to go to such a school, you hopefully know you're privileged.

I've had decent levels of success in my life, but I don't come from a particularly well-off background. It was a big deal for my parents to send me to that school. My dad worked hard, and my mum worked even harder to get me there. I feel lucky to have been able to attend. As you can imagine, there are lots of extremely wealthy people there because it's prestigious and the fees are so high.

Anyway, I glommed onto the idea that a whole bunch of kids from Geelong Grammar were in the audience. I was excited to hear that I would be in front of a hometown crowd. I decided to change up my introduction, do a shout-out to those people, and personalise it for the Geelong Grammar gang.

I thought this small talk would help me connect with the audience, break the ice, and help me feel more at home.

When I walked onto the stage, I realised it was a much bigger audience than I had thought; more like 1,500 people in the audience. And I was taken aback by that. It was a shame I hadn't rehearsed in the room before I walked onto the stage—I'll talk more about how vital it is to rehearse in the space in Chapter 14. That also put me off my stride and, as a result, I doubled down on the Geelong Grammar bit in my introduction. Standing at the lectern, looking out on the sea of expectant faces, I opened with a super upbeat statement:

"It's great to be in a room amongst friends. Especially my friends from Geelong Grammar! Welcome to you all; it's great to see you here."

I waited for the cheers and applause. Instead, there was total silence.

The silence stretched for a beat, and another excruciating beat. I'm pretty sure I saw a tumbleweed rolling along the stage, and then someone called out from the back of the audience, "We're from Geelong College."

If you happen to know Victoria, you might also know Geelong College is a bitter rival to Geelong Grammar. It's a vastly more affordable school. The demographic of students is entirely different. To say they hate the yuppies and rich people who got into Geelong Grammar would be an understatement. And I'd just identified with their natural enemy. It was like walking into a room full of sharks and shouting, "*Go orcas!*"

Within thirty seconds I'd killed the chemistry in the room, and as you can imagine, was completely thrown off my game. It felt like the audience was against me—and you know what, maybe they were. It took me at least the first twenty minutes of that forty-five-minute presentation to recover and get back into the flow of my content, and honestly, I'm not sure I ever quite regained my stride. I would chalk it up as one of my worst presentations ever. But the silver lining is that it was a bloody good lesson that taught me a lot. I probably could have been tighter and looser, so that I could have dealt with that kind of turbulence at the start of the presentation.

The main lesson was: be careful what you do at the start of your presentation. Reaching for that idea of safety resulted in small talk tripping me up.

We've talked about how small talk can be distracting, derail you, and rob you of status in the room.

I want to remind you to run hot while the audience is at its warmest. Better to have an uncomfortable audience wondering what the hell is coming next than a complacent group of people preparing to be bored. Remember that first impressions count for so much that how you open your pitch should be something you focus a disproportionate amount of your preparation time on.

And if you're still worried about making people uncomfortable, I'll talk you through how to ensure you can retain your edge and still be likeable in the next section.

Chapter 3

GET PHYSICAL

"I can do anything when I am in a tutu."
—Misty Copeland

This chapter is about bringing your whole self to the pitch—body and mind.

We tend to think of presenting with confidence as being all in our heads, but the connection between mind and body is so important that I want to take this chapter to show you how working with the body is vital in creating a potent and lasting impression.

By the end of this chapter, you'll be thinking about how to incorporate physical techniques into your public speaking preparation, just as an athlete prepares for a competition. I'll highlight tools and practices that will help you with self-regulation and improve nonverbal communication by fostering a strong mind-body connection. Becoming more comfortable in your body while you're pitching can enhance your confidence and ultimately help you deliver more potent and memorable presentations.

I'll run through a variety of tools I've employed and recommend to my public speaking clients and that you can use to help your body to be at peak readiness. You might find that they're helpful to you in your day-to-day life—that's a bonus.

1. Like a Superhero
2. Inhale the Future, Exhale the Past
3. Change Your Perspective
4. (Don't) Break a Leg
5. Stretch Goals
6. Regulate

If you build even some of these practices into your public speaking preparation, you will notice a significant shift in your self-confidence and the confidence you project to others, and your general ease and enjoyment of the pitch process will increase.

If you've ever done a big keynote or a high-stakes pitch, you'll know it can feel as though you've run a marathon afterwards. I've included some methods to help you calm any pre-pitch nerves and some exercises that will change the way you use your body and improve your nonverbal communication. A deeper dive into body language takes place later in this book.

And, while I am not suggesting that you need to be built like LeBron James or Serena Williams, learning how to get the most out of your body will assist you in reaching your full potential.

It's the foundation of your house. It's the fuel in your car. Get it right and everything else will be that much easier. It's a virtuous cycle in terms of confidence. Feeling more at ease in your body will translate to more confident body language. Whatever we think is how we move, and vice versa. Feeling good helps us think better. While the body can lie, it takes effort, and that can take your focus away from the job you're there to do.

Body language that's congruent with your intentions, and with the content of your speech, is a powerful combination.

Let's talk about getting out of your head and getting into your body. Lots of yogis and meditation practitioners talk about this—and so do sports coaches and professional athletes. A big part of being high-performance is being attuned to your body and your mind.

Cast your mind back to the last time you went into a

pitch, or you went to have an important conversation with a friend, or you went to meet with your boss to ask for a pay rise. You probably spent a lot of time thinking about the words you were going to use; maybe you wrote pages of notes. But did you prepare physically?

In my experience, working with thousands of executives, no one's doing it. That's good news for you, because now you've got another advantage.

I'll work through a few different ways you can limber up and get physical before a presentation. But first, let's talk about why this is important. Well, think about high-performance athletes. They would never go and try and run their personal best, jump their personal best height, or swim their personal best lap without preparation. They stretch, they warm up, and they exercise with a rigorous focus to be high-performance.

Just think about what Tony Robbins does to prepare for a presentation. Granted, Tony has an extremely high-energy presentation style that might be a bit much for your average boardroom, but the underlying lessons of ensuring you're at your peak physical capability still apply, whether you're presenting the latest financial data to a room full of accountants, delivering a eulogy, or working up a crowd of footy players.

Robbins begins his preparation with meditation (using his breath to create physiological and psychological change); he plunges himself into cold water, warms up his voice, and just before going on stage, he jumps rapidly on a trampoline, getting his heart rate up and his blood pumping.

Then, as he takes the stage, he starts clapping wildly,[9] which isn't only giving a signal of excitement to the audience but has also been shown to be one of the most effective ways to get the brain fully online and raring to go. He's not only warm when he begins his presentation, he's also so hot he's already pouring with sweat.

You probably won't be packing a mini-trampoline next time you show up at a meeting, but by understanding the reasons behind his pre-show rituals, we can translate the techniques to our situation.

Need to get out of your head and into your body as quickly as you can? We know that we can change our body chemistry in as little as two minutes through techniques like breathing and posture.

Like a Superhero

Harvard psychologist Amy Cuddy found that "postural expansiveness"—sitting or standing with head up, shoulders back, and chest expanded—had a marked effect on a person's mental and physiological state. Holding a power pose—you might know this as a Wonder Woman pose—for only two minutes made research subjects feel more powerful and confident, and there was also a correlation between lower levels of the stress hormone cortisol and increased levels of testosterone.[10]

---

9 Min Ji Kim, Ji Heon Hong, Sung Ho Jang. "The cortical effect of clapping in the human brain: A functional MRI study." *NeuroRehabilitation*. 2011.

10 Amy J.C. Cuddy, S. Jack Schultz, Nathan E. Fosse. "P-Curving a More Comprehensive Body of Research on Postural Feedback Reveals Clear Evidential Value for Power-Posing Effects: Reply to Simmons and Simonsohn (2017)." *Psychological Science*. 2018.

Inhale the Future, Exhale the Past

Mastering breathing techniques aren't just useful for public speaking. They can be used in any of the situations life throws at you. Whether you're looking to hype yourself up or calm yourself down, breathing is at the core of everything.

As is often said in yoga classes…*the body follows the mind, and the mind follows the breath.*

Pranayama, or breath control, has been used in Eastern traditions for thousands of years. Breathing is one of the few autonomic functions that we can change with conscious effort and directly affects the parasympathetic and sympathetic nervous systems. Not only can it help you manage stress, but some breathing techniques can also help you clear your head and get amped up, albeit not quite to the level of Tony Robbins.[11]

One breathwork power-up is Kundalini breathing. You might have encountered it during yoga classes; it's primarily used for stress relief, although it has plenty of other benefits. Practising this technique at home and prior to a pitch will deliver a better performance.

In a nutshell, you take short panting breaths, pulling your belly to your spine as you exhale and filling your abdomen as you inhale. It's sometimes called the breath of fire, and it's an amazing way to get yourself in the zone before you present.

Navy SEALs use a technique called box breathing,

---

11   Sarah Novotny, Len Kravitz. "The Science of Breathing."

which helps relieve stress and helps you stay calm under pressure. Unlike Kundalini, this technique can be used on stage, as it isn't much different from how most of us breathe normally. You simply inhale, hold, exhale, and hold, making each step of this process last the same number of seconds. I find it's a great way to centre yourself and get present in the room.

Imagine your breath is creating the shape of a box. Breathe in for three (or four) seconds. You hold that breath for three (or four) seconds. You then let the breath out for the same duration. At the bottom of the exhale, hold for the same time again. And around that box, you go. Maybe you want to stretch the timing out, but however you do it, within four or five rounds, you'll feel much more centred, ready to be high-performance when you present.

The key here is that any technique that increases your awareness of your breath and helps you use it consciously will anchor you into your body the second you begin.

For further reading on breathing, I strongly recommend James Nestor's *Breath: The New Science of a Lost Art*.

Nestor's key message is that we need to breathe through our noses as much as possible—mouth breathing has a range of horrible side effects not enough of us are aware of—and the more slowly and less frequently we breathe, the more effective the breath becomes. Fewer breaths per minute mean higher levels of carbon dioxide, which helps optimal oxygen absorption throughout the body.

Nestor also makes the fascinating point that across the world, many religious and spiritual practices share a pacing and rhythm that equates to taking about six breaths per minute. I'll share more about timing and the importance of shifting our pace in the next chapter, but if this practice exists across faiths, across continents, and throughout human history, I reckon it might be worth consideration.

Change Your Perspective

Another way to calm those last-minute nerves is to use our vision. Changing what we're looking at and how frequently we move our gaze can trigger a mechanism that tells our nervous system to stand down, that we're not in immediate danger— remembering that our entire parasympathetic nervous system evolved for an environment where we needed to be ready to run from or fight predators and is often massively out of step with our modern environment.

Shifting your gaze tells the brain we're safe and can move out of hypervigilance into relaxation.

This visual mode is called panoramic vision or optic flow. By keeping your head still, you can dilate your gaze so you're looking into the periphery—above, below, and to the sides. Not only does that tell your brain to chill, but it also gives you a sense of expansive awareness of your surroundings, and this calm centredness is an ideal state for tuning in to your audience as you begin to present.

From my experience, I haven't met a successful public speaker who doesn't warm up (or at least has a routine) before stepping into the light. We have covered some of the breathing techniques to get you focused, but what about your whole body?

(Don't) Break a Leg

Think of your legs as the foundation of your delivery. They are your support and strength, so training and stretching them are key, even if you'll be sitting while presenting. I find lower body exercises are a good way to ground yourself.

During a pitch, if you're sitting straight and upright, your body language can communicate brittleness. Knees, hips, jaw locked—that rigid posture can end up being an easy way to get knocked around in a meeting. One question can bowl you over when you're holding yourself like that.

But if you've done some lower body exercises, for example, squats or stretching your hamstrings, you'll be amazed to find you can feel almost able to grip the ground, to ground yourself in a way where you feel more stable. You feel able to respond to pressure more fluidly, respond to questions on the fly, and more secure and present in the room.

Think of the stance of a martial artist: there's a bounce to the balls of the feet, knees are loose and unlocked. Try thinking about how you're balanced—is your weight evenly distributed across your body? Being alert but also loose and flexible helps you feel ready for anything.

Light stretches (using the breathing techniques outlined earlier), jogging, and walking are all great ways to prepare your body.

Stretch Goals

Above the waist, it's all about using body movement and gesticulation to engage your audience. Our optimum body posture should be open, relaxed, and free moving. Head up, but not so far that you're looking down your nose at your conversation partner. Maintain good eye contact (eye contact is so important that I have written an entire chapter about it). And keep your hands and wrists loose, ready to add gestures to illustrate the points you're making in a way that fits your culture and communication style.

Stretches focusing on decreasing any tension in your shoulders, neck, elbows, and wrists will all help you perform at your optimum level. Your body language is looser and more confident, so you can move around with confidence and command a stage; you can move around and control a small room.

We talked a little about relaxing your jaw in Find Your Voice. It's a part of our body we don't think much about in terms of limbering up, but there are several techniques that can help you produce the widest variety of sounds and improve pronunciation and enunciation. Try using tongue twisters to get your mouth, tongue, and throat all working together.

Regulate

The overarching principle of all these types of exercises is helping regulate your nervous system.

When I'm getting ready to present, even now, there can still be times when I start to go into that old pattern of feeling some anxiety or tension about the thought that I might stutter.

The exercises I've described are things that I use. Breathing, exercising beforehand, and making sure I'm well hydrated. Over the last few years, I've adopted a regular ice bath habit. Cold water exposure has helped me in several ways, both physically and mentally. In the public-speaking world, I can chase down any last-minute jitters that inevitably arise. The mental chatter and excuses start flowing when you stand next to an ice bath, about to get in. Over time you learn to stop negotiating with yourself and *just get in.*

If plunging into an ice bath isn't something you can manage, you can try submerging your face into a basin of cold water (the icier, the better) or use cold packs on your chest, wrists, and neck to stimulate the vagus nerve and help regulate your parasympathetic nervous system.

Breathing, cold water exposure, stretching…they all get your endorphins pumping, bring your awareness back into your body, and stop any negative thoughts from taking over.

We've talked about why you need to use your whole body to help stop all the overthinking and instead start doing well in public speaking.

I believe it's vital to get out of your head and into your body; from my own experience and the people I work with, it's one aspect that makes a huge impact.

Run through the techniques I've outlined and feel how differently you approach the presentation afterwards.

When we walk into the room, inhabiting our bodies, feeling grounded and positive, breathing evenly through our nose, our gaze relaxed, this gives us the feeling of not just being ready to win the room; we're ready to enjoy it.

Chapter 4

PACING AND PAUSING

"It's important for us to pause for a moment and make sure that we are talking with each other in a way that heals, not a way that wounds."

—Barack Obama

This chapter focuses on the speed of your presentation and outlines how to use pacing and pausing to alter the cadence and help your content connect with the audience.

There are two critical reasons to do this: one is for your audience, and the other is for you.

Pacing and pausing are incredibly effective in keeping your audience engaged and conveying confidence. Slowing down the delivery and intentionally incorporating pauses allows the audience time to absorb information, signalling key points in the content, and helps eliminate filler words, thereby creating a more compelling and impactful speech. When you master this technique, it will help you handle unexpected disruptions and give you a greater sense of control, which in turn creates a positive feedback loop.

I'll run through a range of techniques to get you out of the habit of running through the content at ever-increasing speed.

1. Pace Yourself
2. Why the Big Pause?
3. One Breath, One Thought
4. Hold the High-Stakes Moments
5. Pause for Mojo

We all speak too fast when we present to an audience. In all my years of doing Winning the Room training and workshops, I don't believe I've ever come across a person who speaks too slowly.

If you take one thing away from this chapter, it's the need to pump the brakes.

✳✳✳

It's common for public speakers to start at point one, slide one, and then motor through the content until the last point or last slide, gathering speed as we go like a runaway train. It's typical because so many of us don't enjoy the experience of public speaking. Maybe it's even your worst nightmare. So, I guess it's fair enough—why would you want to do anything to make the experience last a second longer than necessary?

Unfortunately, while you might be achieving your goal of getting through the misery as quickly as possible, likely, you're going to miss the mark when it comes to creating an enduring impression on your audience and influencing them to get on board with your big idea. The time you save by racing through your speech is time wasted—yours and your audience's.

Strategically considering the pace of your presentation and where and how you pause are big parts of feeling and being perceived as confident and in command of your content and audience.

Here are a couple of key reasons why.

The first is an audience-based reason. If you talk too fast, your audience cannot absorb what you're saying. This applies to small audiences and gets more important as your audience grows. At a basic level, they can't keep up. When they fall behind and lose their place in your content, they will end up zoning out and drifting away from you.

If it's important to you that your audience engages with your content—which, let's be honest, it should be if you're bothering to public speak—then you've got to get your pace right.

Boredom and disengagement, like many human

emotions, are contagious, and we don't want a single member of our audience to feel this way, let alone watch it spread around the room.

Think about it like this. If you were showing a potential buyer around your home, you wouldn't rush them from room to room, never stopping to have a proper look around. No, you'd start outside and talk about the street and surrounding area, then slowly walk inside the front gate, and begin setting the scene. Once inside, you'd show them each room slowly, taking your time and letting them get a feel for the place, maybe inviting them to sit in your favourite chair or take in the view. You'd make time for them to ask questions. Ultimately, you'd give them the space they need to imagine themselves living in your home. A great public speaker does something similar with their content; timing is critical.

The second reason is for you, the public speaker. Getting your head around timing will give you confidence. Like many of the techniques in this book, the more confident you get, the more you'll allow yourself to slow down; you create your own positive feedback loop. Slowing down and using pauses—even moments of silence—is also a clear signal to the audience that you're so confident you can take all the time in the world; and that you're in control of the rhythm. It's a power move.

Pace Yourself

Let's start with pacing. Not to be confused with speed, pacing is about the rhythm or tempo of your presentation. The more you can plan and control the pace of your presentation, the more confident you will feel, and the more your audience will pay attention.

First, you need to think about what you want to communicate. What are you trying to say without words? For example, a choppy, high-BPM pace tells your audience that you're running through some simple and easy details. No real need to debate or analyse. Just accept it as the widely known truth. This can be the perfect pace to adopt when trying to build energy and momentum.

In contrast, a purposeful and slower pace tells your audience they need to lean right in and pay attention to every word. What you're saying is worth analysis and holds weight. You're subtly telling them there are consequences, and they need to pay attention carefully. This is a great pace to adopt when you're asking for something from your audience, such as money, a discount, an upgrade, or even an agreement.

The key thing about pace is planning it well before you're in the room. Think about pace while you're piecing together what you're going to say. Sometimes you may need to say less because of great pacing. That's because your pace is communicating without words. A golden rule is that if you can say something with fewer words, do it!

Another thing to consider about pace is that you must keep shifting it throughout your presentation. Your pace shouldn't be the same throughout. I like to plan out my pace, so it feels directional, like it's going somewhere. A helicopter view of great pacing might go something like this:

Start slow and purposeful to shift the tone in the room and make people look up and pay attention. Then, as you move from your introduction into the main section of your presentation, maybe you gradually speed up to build excitement and motor through some data and stats. Then, as you get to your main point or idea, you could slow down, probably slower than your intro, to underline this section. This is your moment to let your words linger and sink in. Then, once your idea has landed, maybe you speed up again to get through some easy-to-digest supporting points. Then, at the end, you might slow down again and bring your audience back to where you started, in pace but also in content. You're basically bookending your speech so it feels complete, neat, and resolved.

Why the Big Pause?

As you can imagine, a great way to drive and control pace is to use a close cousin of pacing: pausing. Pausing is a terrific way to create meaningful moments and direct your audience toward what you want them to remember.

I recommend putting pauses before and after each of your major points to get a feel for how powerful pausing can be. It is the quickest way to drive recall. Yes, many other things can be done to make people remember your points, but pausing is the easiest. You will see the results almost immediately.

One Breath, One Thought

A simple way to think about this is "one breath, one thought"—rather than taking a deep breath when you begin a new thought, focus on the out-breath at the end of the thought.

You might be thinking with dismay, "But if I pause and slow down, I'll be speaking for longer!" Why would anyone who hates public speaking want to do that?! Once you get through the fear and pain, you often find comfort and reward on the other side. I love using big pauses when I present and witnessing the rewards every time I do it.

Recently, I was presenting a big, edgy idea to a major car manufacturing client. I'd never met the CEO before, but I had heard that he was conservative.

I used pacing and pausing in that meeting to start a relationship and reassure him that I wasn't going to blow anything up! Every time I paused...he looked up at me. I met him there and showed him with my actions (not words) that I was there to help, not disrupt—even though our ideas were quite disruptive. I'm making a point that we were in a "conversation" during those pauses. No words were exchanged, but we both had ample time to eyeball each other and build trust. He could tell I cared and that I was willing to go at his pace. The meeting went well, and we got full sign-off.

When you pause, your audience will naturally look up at you and listen. If you've lost your audience's attention, a big pause will usually bring them back.

> "That's when you know you've found someone really special. When you can just shut the fuck up for a minute and comfortably share a silence."
>
> —Mia Wallace, *Pulp Fiction*

People aren't always in a meeting to buy what you're selling. They're thinking about their to-do list, what they plan to have for lunch. You need to shake them out of their complacent state of mind, and silence, more than any other tactic, can stop a room of wandering minds.

I like to experiment with this. At times I get up and say nothing. I smile around the room, hold the moment, and feel the tension build. When I finally speak, I can feel the shift, that sense of relief—and the audience now has a clear feeling that they need to pay attention and follow along.

So, you've written your speech, and now you're wondering exactly when and where you should pause.

Hold the High-Stakes Moments

A great way to build a habit of pausing is to mark up your speech notes. I use a simple dot-dot-dot (ellipsis) to show where I intend to pause. I then use this marked-up script for all my rehearsals. I will look through the speech as I do with voice modulation and circle the major points. I also look for anywhere that's about jeopardy or consequences. Basically, moments where the stakes are high, and therefore I want to accentuate those moments and get my audience to think about them.

These are the moments to pause. I recommend a medium pause before and a big pause directly after.

When you pause, a few things happen. Firstly, as a speaker, you get a moment to take in the audience, look around, and enjoy the present moment. That's a real benefit for you and will usually lift your overall confidence and performance. Secondly, your audience gets a moment to think about what you're saying. After a while, this "pause, point, pause" rhythm lets your audience know when major points of interest are coming. When done consistently, you'll start to see your audience lean in at these moments or even pick up their pen in anticipation of something worth writing down.

Not to sound like a control freak, but in a way, you've started to take charge of your audience, or at least the conversation. Maybe it's more like leading in a dance partnership. Either way, you're in control and confidently leading the moment. Importantly, you're doing it at a pace that works for you and your partner (the audience). It also shows that you're in control of the subject matter. You're not rushing and have the confidence to pause during your speech. Rather than madly running from start to finish in your presentation, you're taking the time to pause and let the points sink in. You know what you're talking about and taking the time to help them get across it, too.

The rule is simple. If you want someone to remember something you're about to say, make sure you build up to that moment, pause before you say the point, and pause again after it. I might add, while you're pausing, don't just stand there. This is a prime opportunity for you to use many of the other practical tips in this book. Things like eye contact, body language, props, slides, and facial expressions communicate in an amplified way when they're done during a pause.

Pause for Mojo

Pausing and pacing are also handy techniques to remember when you need to recover from something unexpected that throws you off. Often, our nerves can be at their worst just as we're about to commence, which can lead to a voice that cracks, wavers in tone and pitch, and undermines our confidence. If this happens to you, remember to slow down and breathe. A sip or two of water while you compose yourself can be hugely helpful. Similarly, slowing right down won't necessarily look like you're struggling—in fact, when done with confidence, it can appear that you're in complete control and simply trying to find the perfect words and delivery while you compose your speech on the fly.

If all of that wasn't compelling enough for you to start taking pace and pausing seriously, let me add one final side benefit.

Most people have a few "filler words" that they say often when public speaking. In the trade, they're known as "disfluencies." Commonly those filler words are sounds like "umm," "err," or gravitas-stealing phrases such as "like" and "you know?" We use these types of filler words for many reasons, but the most common reason is nerves. They also allow a speaker to think while considering a question or figuring out what to say next. Unfortunately, they reek of a lack of confidence and disrupt the flow. Nothing kills cred quite like them; they position you as less senior, and the impression for the audience is that you don't know your own content.

Pausing is a great way to eat the um's and err's. Instead of using a filler word, you just pause. I've seen people almost entirely delete their filler words with this technique. It takes practice, but it works.

In a more intimate setting, they allow the speaker to hold the floor and stop others from jumping in. Using pauses can overcome the jarring effect of someone stammering as they try to regain their thread and reestablish credibility and confidence.

I have learned to love silence when I public speak, but more on that in the "Say More with Less" section (Chapter 24).

All these reasons are valid and important. My only request is that you replace these filler words with pauses. This change alone will lift your confidence and increase your chances of being remembered.

Slowing down, altering the pacing of your pitch, and using pauses help you feel confident, show your audience that you are confident, and give you a tool to emphasise the most important points and help you to control the room.

The more I present and the more I watch team members and clients present, the more I realise that nobody pauses enough. Even the biggest pausers in the world do not pause enough. If we're in the attention game, which I have to remind you we are, especially with the world as it is, so jumbled up with information and human noise, we all need to be slowing down to grab and hold attention more often. Pausing is a big way to do just that.

Pacing and pausing are powerful ways of creating that sense of a completely bespoke, personal presentation created specifically for this meeting and the people in the room with you.

Chapter 5

GEAR CHANGING

"That's part of the policy:
to keep switching gears."

—Ridley Scott

Changing gears is like the idea of developing a range. This chapter covers the importance of giving your audience various ways to connect with your concept.

Changing gears during your presentation means varying your presentation style to adapt to the needs of the audience, presenting a range of ideas, and adjusting your energy levels throughout to maintain their attention.

We'll look at some of the brain science behind decision-making that will show you why gear changing in the room is so important and offer some strategies to help you present ideas in a multifaceted and effective way.

The techniques offer simple, actionable ways to switch gears to work with your audience's attention span. Capitalising on how human brains make choices is something I'll cover in more detail as we progress through this book, but for gear-changing, we are focusing on how to adapt your presentation to meet the audience's needs.

1. Six Hats
2. Turning It Up to Eleven
3. Being Your Own Co-Pilot
4. Timing Your Gear Changes

This chapter is about empathising with the audience, understanding their needs and decision-making processes, and tailoring your pitch accordingly.

✳ ✳ ✳

When I started out in advertising, a wise boss once told me I needed to "get some more gears." I had no idea what she meant then, but I've since realised that she was onto something important. She was commenting on how I treated clients and that I was basically the same no matter who the client was. I didn't have enough "gears" or enough of a range of styles. In her opinion, I'd do better if I found different (more bespoke) gears for each client. Naturally, she was right, and I eventually took her advice and expanded my range.

Fast forward to today, and I use this same idea when working with people on their speeches. "Gear changing," as I now call it, has several aspects, and I'll walk through them with you now.

The first aspect is in line with my old boss's feedback. In essence, change your style based on the audience you're speaking with. Sounds bleedingly obvious, but we all tend to be so caught up in our content and—hopefully—now the techniques we're learning together in this book that we forget about our overall style. When did you last make an intentional gear shift in a conversation or a presentation? I would imagine not often. I encourage you to think a lot more about changing up your style.

We've talked about the need to be your authentic self and to anchor your confidence in self-belief, but paradoxically this section focuses on adapting your style for your audience.

While it appears to be in direct conflict with "being your authentic self," bringing the range to your presentation style brings more nuance, rather than obdurately sticking to your guns no matter what.

A moment where the chameleon wins all.

Whilst we might have crafted a persona for ourselves, we are all capable of a lot more depth and range than a personal branding expert might like to deal with. So don't get stuck in your predominant gear—explore and develop the others, so you strengthen your range and ability to relate to different personalities. It will help you not just in public speaking but in life! You might have a reputation as a tough, uncompromising rationalist, or you may be exceptionally skilled in building rapport with a softer style, but either of these personas is going to leave you high and dry if you find yourself presenting to someone who doesn't gel with that mode of expression. Bringing a multifaceted presentation style will give you much more flexibility and options in the room.

Good communication, no matter what form it takes, considers the needs of the audience first and foremost. So, think about your audience. What do they want? What will make them engage with you? What will make them believe you? What do you want them to feel from you?

Once you consider some of these possibilities, I highly recommend changing gears and addressing them with your presentation style.

What we're talking about is showing empathy for our audience. We can't know what their dominant characteristics are or what their decision-making processes are like. Our modern world is highly mobile, and that means often we're in contact with people whose context or background is unlike our own. Even if you happen to be presenting to someone you know or have worked with in the past, you can't know what kind of day they're having.

The process of decision-making is notoriously erratic. We are generally a lot less rational than we believe ourselves to be. Research into the affect heuristic[12] shows us that decision-making is heavily influenced by our current mood—if we're feeling good, we're more receptive to new ideas and taking risks, whereas if we're having a bad day, we're less open to novel information and more likely to say no to a pitch.

By demonstrating range and creating several routes into our big idea, we're giving our audience a choice of pathways to reach the ideal destination.

I recently coached a team from a large apparel business. They were about to go on a national roadshow to sell their new sustainable fabrics to existing clients. The new fabric was revolutionary—but had a higher cost per unit. On a factual level, it should have been an easy yes. The plan they came to me with was a logical one. They would talk about the environmental benefits (they had lots of statistics) and compare their products to the less sustainable alternatives on the market. That approach would doubtless have connected with those clients who already deeply cared about the environment. But what about clients who were apathetic? Or clients who didn't want to pay the higher prices for sustainable materials?

We reworked the presentation and used an effective gear change to transform their rational pitch into an emotional one.

The pitch started out celebrating the clients' breadth and depth in apparel production. This is exactly what any of their clients would expect. We detailed their scale and showed just how successful they'd become in terms of garments made.

---

12   Melissa L. Finucane, Ali Alhakami, Paul Slovic, Stephen M. Johnson. "The affect heuristic in judgments of risks and benefits." *Journal of Behavioral Decision Making*. 13:1–17. 2000.

We then gear changed to the idea of responsibility. In essence, we asked them a simple question: "What responsibility comes with this level of success?" With high-impact visuals, we then demonstrated the apparel industry's role in "trashing the planet" and then, for the first time, we mentioned the new sustainable fabric line. A fabric line for clients that have achieved success and now understand their responsibility.

I was lucky enough to sit in on a few of the presentations, and the results were obvious. Everyone in the audience looked up and leaned forward as soon as the gear change happened. By the end of the meeting, the discussion was about *how* they could incorporate the new product instead of *if* they should in the first place.

Six Hats

One way to do this is to employ a technique Edward de Bono coined in the 1980s called the "Six Thinking Hats," where you approach the problem from several perspectives. This is a process you'd do at the rehearsal stage, and just as you've learned to do in preparing your strategic small talk, you choose to present some or all these options, depending on your reading of the room (more on this later) and which gear you feel you need to move into.

The perspectives range from the rational to the optimistic, from a pessimistic outlook to lateral and creative solutions to a gut feeling or emotive response to the issue.

Research shows that humans are surprisingly poor at assessing other people's thinking. This means most of us are unlikely to gauge how receptive our audience is and therefore need to have a range of gears we can switch to, based on the live response we get in the room. I'll go deeper into reading the room in Chapter 12.

These gear shifts could mean that you go from telling a heartfelt story about how the solution you're pitching would change lives, to a more humorous pitch, perhaps with a note of self-deprecation, to a strategic or analytical perspective.

When you combine this ability to shift gears with the skills we will cover in more depth—reading the room, body language, and others—you're giving yourself an impressive toolkit. I've seen people so focused on getting through their slides in the room that they miss the moment when the audience leans in, ready to buy, looking for a shift in tone and gear to make getting to that "yes" a foregone conclusion.

Turn It Up to Eleven

The second aspect is more about how your energy levels evolve and flow within your speech. Many people I coach want to dial up their energy levels when presenting. So much so, they often start presenting at a ten in energy and then try to maintain that level throughout their speech.

Not only is that exhausting for you, the presenter, but it's also exhausting and hard to engage with the audience. You've got to give yourself somewhere to go. My advice is simple: start your introduction at a six on the energy scale and slowly ramp it up during your presentation so you can end on a surprising ten—or maybe drop it right down to a whispered one!

Change your gears up and down depending on the point

you're making for bonus points and even more cut-through. Maybe you start at a four and then move up to an eight, back down to a six, then up to a nine, and so on. Always keeping your audience engaged and along for the ride. Going back to our F1 analogy, hopefully, as you hone your skills, you can drive that performance sportscar according to the changing conditions you find yourself facing on the day.

Be Your Own Co-Pilot

How does one do clever gear changes? Well, it starts with planning your presentation. Think of this like driving a rally car with a brilliantly intelligent co-pilot on board. That person will have plotted the course, marked up the map, and worked out how to take each corner or hairy bend without losing ground well before you ever turn the key in the ignition.

You need to think about who you are talking to and what you will say and find appropriate moments to change gears accordingly.

I recommend writing those gear changes in the margins or notes section to make it clear and easy to follow. That way, when you rehearse, you can refer back. And you're blending this gear change in with the changes you're mapping out in terms of your pacing and pausing, as well as the voice modulation you now know is critical to keeping the audience engaged.

Time Your Gear Changes

As a basic guideline, I'd aim for a deliberate gear change two to three times in a twenty-minute presentation. If your pitch is sixty minutes long, you will need at least six gear changes in your presentation, designed around critical moments in your content.

Your audience will consciously or subconsciously notice these moments of change, and it will naturally draw them deeper into your content, giving you more ways to connect with your audience on different levels.

Gear-changing is a technique to help you connect with people in whatever mode you find them in. Planning gear changes in advance give you a solid and adaptable framework for your public speaking moment, helps the audience stay on the side, and gives them more routes into the idea.

Using these techniques—practising in advance and then, in parallel with more of the tools I'll detail in the following chapters—gives you a flexible and fluid set of points to offer and keeps the attention focused on you throughout your presentation.

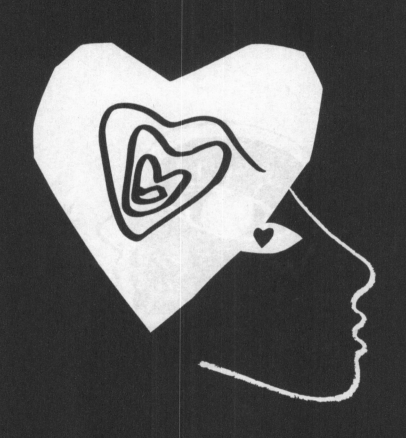

Likeable

SECTION II

People want to do business with people they like. The rest is merely accounting.

This section will explore the *L* for *Likeable* in the CLAIM model.

Your success or failure as a public speaker often depends on whether the audience likes you. I know this sounds trite, but it can be that simple.

It also feels slightly out of your control. After all, it's hard to force people to like you. When it does happen, it usually feels like a natural occurrence.

Think about some of the people you like. Can you describe what made you like them when you first met them? I imagine it's hard to articulate.

Likeability is nothing new, and we usually strive for it in many areas of our lives, generally subconsciously. But I want to discuss in this section the need for likeability when presenting and in business more broadly. In all my years of working with executives, I rarely meet people who think of being likeable in how they present themselves at work as a skill they can work on. It's just something people don't plan or design for.

First, I want you to understand that being likeable to your audience is critical—you need your audience to engage with you and genuinely like you to believe and remember you. And this judgment about your likeability is usually made in the first moments of your presentation. Think about the last person you met—whether you were at a dinner party, in a business meeting, or as an audience member, you decided whether you liked the person in an instant. So, making a quick, positive first impression is critical to good public speaking.

Notions of "hoping for the best" or letting the content

shine through might be proxies. But allowing your natural personality—free from fear—to shine through is usually what matters most when winning the room. So, the question is: can you pitch, present, or public speak in a way that allows your natural personality to come through, in a way that makes you more likeable?

As you'll notice throughout this book, there are two dimensions to most of the CLAIM attributes: the act of being likeable, and then the way that we demonstrate, or "do," likeability. This is another of those potentially uncomfortable considerations. I'm not suggesting that you're not likeable or that you must go away and have a long hard look at yourself. Still, I'm offering you my perspective, gained from speaking to thousands of executives and high-performance teams: people often leave their likeable selves at the door and begin performing a version of professionalism that unintentionally disconnects them from their audience.

We aren't always as good as we imagine at reading social cues, and we're often terrible at putting into practice the behaviours that signal our intentions and feelings to others. Psychologists call this "signal amplification bias"—we assume that other people are picking up what we're putting down, and often this isn't the case. Especially at times of stress—and public speaking is often such a time—we don't communicate effectively, and we're equally likely to misunderstand other people also making these assumptions.

If you're reading this book, you're unlikely to live on a remote island somewhere removed from modern-day society. Your reality, like mine, involves being bombarded by messages all day, every day, from all angles, all the time.

Some you will be conscious of, while others take up space in your subconscious, adding to the noise and clutter of your mind and therefore, your world.

To give you a data-informed view of this situation: it's estimated that the average person is "served" approximately ten thousand advertising messages a day. It sounds wild, but think about it. You only need to look at your phone, turn on the TV, or even walk outside, and you'll be pitched at by someone trying to sell you something—an opinion, a product, a service, an idea, or a belief. We have information coming at us from brands, governments, charities, churches, celebrities, influencers, family, friends, and random strangers…and it's become overwhelming.

Also, most people in the professional world must stay connected to multiple digital platforms, with a proliferation of messages, emails, calls, video conferences, tweets, and so on. We think of ourselves as expert multitaskers because we continually shuffle between activities. Still, neuroscientists tell us that what's happening is that we're quite likely to be inefficient and overly stressed out—the more competing priorities we have, the more cortisol (the stress hormone) is likely to be present.

We're also likely to be developing a low-key addiction to completing non-urgent, irrelevant, or trivial tasks at the expense of what we need to do. Because we get a little dopamine hit when we see a notification or send a tweet, our brain begins to prioritise those activities. The reward centre belongs to the limbic system, the survival-focused part of the brain. While that part of our brain is essential for day-to-day life, it isn't where advanced or analytical thought lives.

Moreover, it won't help you dream up your next big idea or win a pitch. We are so distracted and in a state of nerve-jangling overstimulation that considering how we come across to others is often the last on our overloaded to-do lists.

Humans are tribal creatures, and most of our behaviours are driven by a primal need for belonging and connection—but our brains, paradoxically, aren't always helpful in achieving this. Hardwired to keep us safe, our brains also perceive any possibility of rejection as tantamount to a physical threat. We're so tuned in to the possibility of rejection that, as one study showed, if a stranger didn't make eye contact with the research participants, it genuinely ruined their day, leaving them feeling ostracised and disconnected.[13]

Thinking about whether we're liked by others can hit our deepest darkest fears and make us feel tense and anxious—which is, in turn, going to affect how likeable we are. One of the characteristics people think of as likeable is being relaxed, fun, and easy to spend time with.

Let's work through a few things to be aware of, attributes that amplify your natural personality and make you likeable quickly and instinctively and start using some solid techniques to show our authentically likeable natures to the best effect.

It's perhaps not surprising that research found that liking others was one of the main factors in likeability. Likeable people like people. We also tend to like people who are similar to us. That doesn't mean faking interest or pretending to be peas in a pod—it's about finding ways of identifying similar

13   John B. Nezlek, Eric D. Wesselmann, Ladd Wheeler, Kipling D. Williams. "Ostracism in Everyday Life." *Group Dynamics Theory Research and Practice.* 2012. www.researchgate.net/publication/232566435_Ostracism_in_Everyday_Life.

attributes and values in common or shared interests.

In other words, when we demonstrate openness, we are more likely to be perceived as likeable because we're seen as more likely to accept new perspectives. And it's a self-fulfilling prophecy because, when we're curious and open to others, we ultimately are more likely to accept them for who they are.

Another key attribute of likeable people is being supportive. Instead of framing our interaction as "What can this person do for me?" think about what you can do for them. Keep asking the question, "How can I add value for my audience?" This mindset of adding value is a game-changer, and I'll dive deeper into this in Chapter 11. For now, keep in mind that a generous mindset can change your delivery, content, and overall outcome.

Another attribute of likeable people is to be curious. A great way to show your curiosity is to ask interesting and strategic questions (never small talk, though!) that make it apparent to the audience that you care, that you want to hear what they have to say, and that you're engaged. Being interested is more important than being interesting.

Empathy is another key quality of likeable people, and again, one of the best ways to demonstrate this is to listen. Research shows that, while active listening is a predictor of organisational success,[14] personally and professionally, we are collectively unskilled at the art of doing it:[15] As a human race, this was once our strength. For example, for the First Nations

---

14   Jan Flynn, Tuula-Riitta Valikoski, Jennie Grau. "Listening in the Business Context: Reviewing the State of Research." *International Journal of Listening*. 2008. doi. org/10.1080/10904010802174800.

15   D. Rane. "Good Listening Skills Make Efficient Business Sense." *IUP Journal of Soft Skills*. Dec 2011.

people of Australia, *dadirri*,[16] or deep listening, is the practice of deep and respectful listening, which is essential for building community. Listening without judgment is an important skill to master, and working on this skill is a lifelong pursuit that will undoubtedly benefit other areas of your life.

Ask open-ended questions. Open questions (rather than questions that would give you yes or no answers) demonstrate curiosity and are likely to result in answers with more depth; in turn, this sparks greater curiosity and willingness to listen. Positive reinforcement, and another way to build relevance. Talking to someone else about themselves—or, in our context, about their challenges with this project, goals, or objectives in their role—will help you build relevance, create connection, and make you more likeable.

Another cast-iron tip for building rapport and becoming more likeable—especially if you suspect the other person may not be your biggest fan—is to ask them to do you a favour. It seems counterintuitive, and it's a cognitive bias known as the Benjamin Franklin effect. Essentially, it's the brain's way of avoiding inner conflict or cognitive dissonance: by doing someone a favour, we become invested in their success, partly because it reflects on our status and partly because, by doing them a favour, we rationalise that they must be favour-worthy, and thus likeable.

We will talk more about authenticity later, but it's crucial that the audience or your conversation partner feels you're the real you—not hiding something or using incongruent words and body language.

16 *Dadirri* is from the Ngan'gikurunggurr and Ngen'giwumirri languages of the Aboriginal people of the Daly River region.

It's a fact of life in our superficial world that better-looking people are thought of as more likeable. We can't change how we look, but we can pay attention to how we present ourselves, our affability, and our confidence. If you know you tend to have a touch of "resting bitch face," make a real effort to keep your facial muscles engaged and aim for a smile rather than letting your face collapse into your usual scowl.

Research also shows that physical touch can make us more likeable. I saw the true power of this kind of communication when I spent time with some NLP (neuro-linguistic programming) folks. I won't dive into the details here but, safe to say, a handshake executed whilst holding the other person's elbow communicates loudly!

Haptics is an important part of nonverbal communication, but consensual touch may be acceptable or completely outrageous in the workplace, depending on your culture and context. Needless to say, being respectful of other people's personal space and understanding socially acceptable boundaries are paramount on this one.

One of the outcomes that I have noticed as I've taught people the techniques in this book is this: if you can give your audience this gift of listening, making them feel heard, they want to spend time with you. As I say, you don't need to be all jazz hands and tap shoes, but you can be entertaining and make them feel good and invigorated.

Being jovial—I'll talk more about the art of self-deprecation, but by being relaxed by nature, you yourself stop fretting about your content and start being more present. And it's this magic moment when you start to feel playful, tuned in, and present when public speaking starts to become addictive.

This section will take you through six techniques that will help you demonstrate and amplify your personality in a natural and likeable way when you are public speaking.

Chapter 6

GIVE EYE CONTACT

"Don't believe everything you hear.
Real eyes, realize, real lies."

—Tupac Shakur

Eye contact is a hot wire to likeability. When done well, eye contact reveals the true intent of a presentation and a person. This transparency establishes a real and fast connection between the speaker and the audience.

Naturally, with transparency comes some healthy doses of vulnerability. Therefore, many people I work with struggle with eye contact. In fact, many actively avoid it.

Eye contact helps you physically and energetically connect with your audience. It projects confidence and credibility in what you are trying to communicate. Getting it right matters because a lack of eye contact is not only unengaging but can be viewed as a sign of weakness, dishonesty, or submissiveness. It's a powerful and symbolic way to demonstrate the human warmth and connection we innately crave. If we can meet the eyes of our audience, if we can we do so without faltering, without curling up in a tiny ball, we can show ourselves in our full, likeable—maybe even loveable—glory.

This chapter focuses on the importance of eye contact and what happens from a neurological and physiological standpoint when we make eye contact. I'll share some techniques for putting this into practice in any setting—Zoom In is specifically for eye contact over video calls.

1. Shift Your Gaze
2. Start Small
3. Share the Wealth
4. No Passengers
5. Zoom In

✳ ✳ ✳

An old public speaking tip says you should look directly over the top of your audience's heads. You're not looking into their eyes; you're looking slightly above them. People tend to love this tip because it dilutes the moment for the presenter and allows them to feel less nervous. But at what expense? I'm here to tell you that your audience knows. They can tell. They don't feel connected. There's also nothing more distracting for the audience than someone fixing their gaze on something out of their field of vision.

Have you ever tried the prank where you just stare fixedly at someone's ear or the side of their head just to see how off-balance it gets them? The other person will start self-consciously rubbing their ear or trying to wipe away the invisible smudge on their face because your eyes signal to them that something weird is going on. Imagine the result of doing this to a room full of people. It's the opposite of creating a connection, and apart from anything else, it makes you far less likeable.

Even if you're feeling nervous, try not to focus solely on audience members you know or who appear most responsive. It can seem easier, but everyone in your audience deserves attention.

And please, don't read off your slides or cue cards. You are there to humanise the message and to make a live connection. Text-to-speech software is cheap and readily available, and your audience is literate, so there is no need to stand there and read to them. If you think you'll need to read it, you may want to consider sending them the presentation by email, along with a voice memo, and stay at home. Harsh but true!

Renowned sci-fi director Ridley Scott loves an eye close-up. He uses it in two of his most iconic films, *Blade Runner* and *Alien: Covenant*, and both times, the close-up is revealed to be of the eyes of an android. (Spoilers! Sorry!) Similar close-ups are used in Stanley Kubrick's *2001: A Space Odyssey*, Rian Johnson's *Looper*, and a host of other iconic sci-fi films.

The focus on the eye in such sci-fi films symbolises the importance of humanity, emotion, and connection. We're predisposed (or conditioned) to revere the human elements and reject the robotic. So, just like in these films, eye contact during your presentation can be the difference between being perceived as an engaging, thoughtful, and empathetic speaker who people innately like and want to engage with, versus a mindless or robotic automation reciting a script that they'll be preconditioned to ignore and forget.

Think of eye contact as creating a moment of connection. Every person (depending, of course, on the size of your audience) should share a moment with you. Not only will it help you read your audience and see what is and isn't resonating with them—and I'll get deeper into this in Chapter 12, "Reading the Room"—it will help increase interaction and questions/comments. It's so important.

It's not about talking to a group. It's about talking with a group of individuals. And there's a key difference here: you want to have a one-on-one conversation with a bunch of people. One of the best ways to make this happen, to create that feeling, is to have great eye contact.

You know what it's like when someone is talking to you, but they're not looking at you. They're not looking into your eyes. It's disconcerting, and it feels insincere. You wonder if the person is actually paying attention. And suddenly, when you're talking to them, if they're not looking at you, you start to wonder if anything's even getting across to them. Because of our evolutionary hardwiring to over-index how much we constantly search for possible threats—and because the thought of being rejected feels like a threat to our survival—this can send the threat receptors of our brain into a tailspin.

Try this simple experiment: sit opposite a friend or colleague and run an exercise where one of you tells a story while the other actively tries not to have eye contact with the presenter. Look down, look away—look anywhere but into your conversation partner's eyes. You'll be surprised at how annoying and unengaging it is for the presenter and the partner.

Now try it the other way around: Tell your story without looking at your friend or colleague; instead, look over their head, around the room…anywhere but at them. See what it feels like. You'll find that the person receiving the story will not feel engaged. Their comprehension and recall will also be low. For you, the presenter, you'll also feel disengaged and probably unsure about the success or failure of the conversation.

This is just an exercise; maybe you're writing it off as extreme compared to a real-life situation. I don't think so. I have sat in countless meetings where eye contact has been almost non-existent, and as a result, the connection has been similar.

There is some interesting scientific research on this subject matter. There is a theory that eye contact and tracking where other people are looking is so important that the human eye evolved to make our gaze easier to read—this is why the whites of our eyes are so large compared with other mammals. Fascinating, isn't it?

The novelist Barbara Kingsolver wrote that "humans love things mostly with our eyes," and whether you're a highly visual person or prefer to take in information through other senses, the eyes have it when it comes to emotional connection.

One that stood out to me is a piece of research about the processing of the gaze. Two Canadian researchers set out to test the importance of eye contact in producing "arousal enhancement"[17] in individuals. Minds out of the gutter now, arousal enhancement (in this instance) is a measure of the level of a person's psychological and physical activation. So, for our purposes, think of it as their engagement level.

They tested it by having two people speak to each other in three different scenarios: in the first, the participants were blindfolded; in the second, they were wearing sunglasses; and in the third, they were making direct eye contact. The researchers then measured the skin's conductivity, or electrodermal response, to determine the levels of arousal/engagement (when aroused by something, your skin momentarily becomes a better conductor of electricity). And what do you know? They found that eye contact (and not the actual content of the message) was the major driver of arousal/engagement.

Part of what we're doing when we're public speaking—

---

17 Michelle Jarick, Renee Bencic. "Eye Contact Is a Two-Way Street: Arousal Is Elicited by the Sending and Receiving of Eye Gaze Information." *Frontiers in Psychology*. June 2019. www.frontiersin.org/articles/10.3389/fpsyg.2019.01262/full.

in gear-changing, body language, etc.—is creating moments of change. Arousal or engagement starts to drop when things continue at the same pace and intensity; eye contact is another weapon in the arsenal to grab and keep our audience's attention.

Shift Your Gaze

One of the fastest ways to get people to pay attention is to shift your gaze suddenly.[18] We detect this change almost unconsciously, and it will disrupt the energy in the room immediately. Remembering that our brains evolved to be constantly alert for threats or opportunities, you can tap into that mechanism to shift focus.

One group of researchers also found that when we make direct eye contact,[19] people are more likely to believe us. We are even considered smarter if we hold eye contact for longer. One study showed that people who frequently broke eye contact to move their gaze away from their conversation partner[20] were seen as less intelligent by the research participants, with no other basis for this.

It's possible to go too far with eye contact. Holding it for too long can turn a moment into an eternity: it can feel creepy, aggressive, and charged.

18   Robrecht P. van der Wel, Timothy Welsh, Anne Böckler. "Talking heads or
     talking eyes? Effects of head orientation and sudden onset gaze cues on
     attention capture." *Attention, Perception, & Psychophysics*. 2018. link.springer.
     com/article/10.3758/s13414-017-1462-y.

19   Helene Kreysa, Luise Kessler, Stefan R. Schweinberger. "Direct Speaker Gaze
     Promotes Trust in Truth-Ambiguous Statements." *PLoS ONE*. Sept 2016. doi.
     org/10.1371/journal.pone.0162291.

20   R. Wade Wheeler, Joan C. Baron, Susan Michell, Harvey J. Ginsburg. "Eye contact
     and the perception of intelligence." *Bulletin of the Psychonomic Society*. 1979.
     link.springer.com/article/10.3758/BF03335025.

There is a famous social experiment in which strangers meeting on a blind date have to work through a series of thirty-six questions designed to create a powerful sense of intimacy. The icing on the cake is that, at the end of the questions, they must maintain eye contact with each other for four minutes. Try it with a friend or partner and notice how it feels—four minutes can feel like an unbearably long time to hold a gaze. If you're feeling close, it can build a more intimate sense of connection, but if you've got unresolved issues with one another, or you're in the middle of a fight, it can feel wildly uncomfortable.

While the research I mentioned indicates that eye contact can be powerfully persuasive, there's also some data to support the idea that overdoing it can make it harder for people to retain new information,[21] possibly because we're so busy trying to make sense of the stare that we don't have the cognitive capacity to process and store content.

Overly long stares—and we're talking ten-plus seconds here—can be interpreted as an attempt to dominate or intimidate. And, of course, there are different norms in different cultures—what might be an appropriate duration in the US, for example, could be seen as incredibly invasive and rude in certain Asian countries.

I'll talk more about how you can learn to read the room, but as a general principle, you need to adapt and personalise everything in this book to your style and context.

There is a phenomenon that I think is worth mentioning.

---

21 Dezso Nemeth, Adam Balint Turcsik, Gabriella Farkas, Karolina Janacsek. "Social Communication Impairs Working-Memory Performance." *Applied Neuropsychology. Adult.* 2013. pubmed.ncbi.nlm.nih.gov/23445454.

Some social scientists believe that the amount of eye contact we consider normal has dropped quite dramatically over the past couple of decades because we've become so used to breaking away to check our phones. This behaviour is so common that it's been nicknamed "phubbing."[22] At the risk of sounding like a Luddite, I don't think the way we're allowing technology to disrupt moments of human connection is doing us any favours.

The rise of video conferencing also underpins this idea. When the COVID-19 pandemic was at its height, people began to experience "Video Call Fatigue." One aspect is that we instinctively want to make eye contact with colleagues and clients but have no means to do this on a call.

It's a weird beast. You can either look into the person's eyes on your screen, which means from their point of view you're looking away, or you can stare into the little green dot of your webcam, which means you can't focus on the other person and risk missing important cues from their facial expressions and body language. There's almost no way to get that biofeedback that eye contact in real life gives us.

You could try making the VC window smaller and positioning it nearer to your camera, reducing the gap between the person's image and your camera, but there is no perfect solution yet.

I'm not sure that the AI Deepfake tools that generate a version of your image onscreen that appears to be looking attentively into the camera at all times are the answer. It seems

22   Brandon T. McDaniel, Eric Wesselmann. "'You phubbed me for that?' Reason given for phubbing and perceptions of interactional quality and exclusion." *Human Behavior and Emerging Technologies*. July 2021. onlinelibrary.wiley.com/doi/epdf/10.1002/hbe2.255.

likely to me that it will intensify our feeling of dissonance and disconnection because something will feel "off," but we won't quite understand why.

I hope I've convinced you that eye contact is crucial. But how do you learn to do it well?

Start Small

Like everything I share with you, you'll need to practice. Try speaking about a favourite topic (so the content comes easily to you) to a small, familiar audience, and then gradually increase its size. Family members, housemates, colleagues, and friends are ideal, as this will lessen your nerves and better prepare you for an audience of strangers. Then experiment, give them huge amounts of eye contact, and see how it feels for you and them. Then try smaller amounts, and so on.

Share the Wealth

I want to reframe this for you. Rather than thinking about this as though you're reluctantly dragging your eyes up from the safety of the lectern, think about it like this: When it comes to eye contact, you want to be like Santa Claus at Christmas, although even the naughty kids get their share on this occasion.

You're offering your attention to all audience members, inviting them to share a moment with you, no matter how fleeting.

Think of it as sharing or "giving" someone eye contact, as a gift, rather than the implication of an unwelcome intrusion that the phrase "make" eye contact can subliminally suggest. Human connection is a gift, and one of the ways we create and demonstrate connection is through eye contact.

When it comes to selecting which audience member to focus on next, it's important that you don't have a system in place, marking off each audience member like someone crossing off numbers on a bingo card. Instead, spread your attention like confetti in the wind! It should appear organic, not programmed, and nor should your attention to audience members seem too frantic or scrambled, with your eyes darting from one person to the next. Try not to make it mechanical. Some eye contact is better than none, but there is an optimal way to do this.

There is a mindset behind eye contact, and that mindset is generosity.

You need to give eye contact with an attitude of generosity foremost in your mind. How can you be generous with the eye contact that you're giving out? As you can probably imagine, that's about giving everybody eye contact and ensuring each person gets a generous dose.

The optimal way to do eye contact is to look at individuals, not groups. Look at each person and dwell there, holding their gaze, being present with them, until you get a little bit of feedback. It's often a micro expression, a little smile, or a nod. Once you get that acknowledgment, you can move on to the next person.

This is the key: It's deliberate. It's generous. It's a moment of true connection.

Take your time. Wait until someone's giving you a signal that says, "Yeah, I'm with you!"

You have a moment of exchange: you look at one

another and think, "Yes, I'm with you too; this is fun." Then you move on to the next person. You want to keep these moments feeling natural, unforced, and organic.

Dwell with people for different amounts of time. Maybe you can make a whole point to one individual in the crowd, then you move away. Make another point and, as you make it, spread your eye contact back and forth between four or five people. And then you come back to another person, giving them eye contact for a smaller amount of time. Then you finish the point by making eye contact with someone else.

The key takeaway here is that it's got to feel organic and live. It can't feel mechanical, methodical, or planned out. It's got to feel generous and spontaneous. Try using words like "lavish," "abundant," and "plentiful" as you're reminding yourself to do this (inside voice, you don't need to say this aloud), or if you're a visual thinker, picture yourself like Oprah, exuberantly scattering eye contact like prizes. "You get some eye contact! And you get some eye contact!"

Now, not only is eye contact great for making that connection and feeling of presence as you're talking to each individual person in the audience, but it's also got some amazing side benefits.

No Passengers

Using lots of eye contact lets your audience know that this is a participatory presentation or conversation, and you're setting an expectation that you want them to be involved. In Chapter 15, "Putting the Audience on Notice," we investigate this type of thinking.

In short, the message is this is not a meeting or a conversation where people can float along, check out, and be a passenger. It's going to be participatory: everyone's involved.

If you think about any experience in your life when people reach out to you directly and get you involved, get you talking—that's when you're engaged, and those are the moments you remember. The forgettable moments are when you're just one of the people in the audience when the presentation feels like it's not for you.

The second benefit is that you find out if people understand and engage with your content. And if they're not, you have the opportunity to adjust; you get to read the room and adapt your content.

If you're giving generous eye contact, and you notice someone looking confused or disinterested or even looking down at their phone, you can hang with that person. You can check in and ask them at that moment, "Hey, is this interesting? Is this making sense? You look like you may have a question."

The intention here is not to call them out but to engage with them with these types of welcoming, open questions (we'll dive deeper into this in the next chapter).

You can do this with your body language or even more minimally with your facial movements. Even the tiniest intimation with your eyes: look at them in a way that says, "Hey, are you with me?" And you know, nine times out of ten, they'll give you their attention and presence: "I am here; I'm with you."

And if they don't—great, now is the moment to address it. At first, this assertion may seem awkward or even rude.

But if you don't address it immediately, you're not truly communicating and, therefore, wasting their time and yours. What's ruder?

Think of an alternative scenario where you don't look at your audience, you don't check in, and you don't know if what you're saying is transmitting across to them.

If they're looking down, maybe it's because they've got a question, but they're not bold enough to put their hand up. But if you've got great eye contact, you'll know, and you can reach out to them and have a dialogue, a proper conversation. And that is the ultimate way to connect with people, to grab and hold their attention.

Zoom In

As so many presentations are via video calls these days, I think it is worth addressing eye contact, specifically in a virtual setting.

My advice for reducing video call fatigue and making eye contact on video calls, by the way, is to make deliberate eye contact with the camera at the key points while you're speaking, perhaps at the beginning and the end, and during your pitch at the moments you want to have the most impact. You also need to do this intermittently while the other person is talking, particularly when they're sharing something important, or when they're giving you feedback. Every moment of eye contact with the camera is like punctuation. Use it wisely. And because this can be exhausting and stressful to the nervous system, I would try reducing the number of video calls you make daily.

Keep them for important decision-making situations, and when people try to book meetings into your diary, be certain that the agenda merits a face-to-screen-to-face interaction and couldn't be handled via a phone call or an email.

Remember that our objective is to have an individual one-on-one conversation with a crowd of people. That's the ultimate goal. The side benefits of eye contact are that you can read the room to check in with people to make sure they're involved and adjust your tone or pacing to what the audience needs.

Eye contact can be disconcerting at first, but—as with many of these tips and techniques and fundamentals—once you push through, it becomes fun, and it's rewarding. You're getting immediate feedback; it becomes more fun.

You're communicating likeability by learning to stay present with great eye contact.

While it might feel complex, actually, it's simple.

It comes down to breathing and eye contact. That's a sensational way to be present—and I'm using that word purposefully.

Experience that moment through all your senses by being in your body and feeling 100 percent alive.

People who give you the sense of being present and immersed in the moment you're sharing are the people you remember. You hear it about great leaders: people who made me feel like I was the only person in the room—eye contact is integral to building that connection.

Give it a go. It'll change your public speaking world. It'll change the rest of your world.

Chapter 7

GET THEM TALKING

"It's hard to resist a generous question."

—Krista Tippett

There's a popular misconception about public speaking: the idea that it's a one-way presentation. Most people think public speaking is about you as the presenter and your pitch, and I want to bust this myth. My position is that it still needs to be a real conversation, which, of course, needs multiple speakers—you *and* your audience.

This chapter focuses on building a conversational dynamic that gets the audience engaged and feeling like they're participants, not bystanders. I'll explain why this is crucial to the success of your presentation and outline some of the psychological and neurological reasons behind it. We'll discuss the human brain's negativity bias and tendencies to try to conserve energy by jumping to conclusions and suggest ways to overcome these barriers.

I'll outline some techniques:

1.   The Two-Minute Rule
2.   Five to One
3.   The Opener
4.   Parking Station

These will all help you get your audience talking and make sure the conversation flows as an integral part of your presentation.

***

Setting up a two-way conversation, a two-way pitch, where you present and they present back to you with questions, comments, and feedback, live and in the moment, is critical to creating an engaging and memorable presentation. Presenting, pitching, and talking the whole time, in a one-way flow of ideas and information from you to your audience, will not be effective. You need to speak, and you also need to listen, and the questions you ask and the way you engage matter a great deal. We don't want to lean into inconsequential chit-chat—death to small talk, remember?—but rather to get the conversation partner or your audience to discuss the subject matter. Pulling the audience into the experience, getting them to engage, process the information, and add value.

We are performers, moving the audience through a live experience.

Trends on TikTok come and go, but one from a while ago that stuck with me was "main character energy." It's a vivid way to express the idea that, rather than being a supporting cast member in your life, you need to pull focus and step into the spotlight of your existence. It's a cool way to frame it; many people need that nudge.

However, when it comes to your pitch—and I realise this may sound contradictory—it's not about you. This section is about putting the audience on the spot and getting them to engage and exchange value with you. This is strategic for a few reasons:

We talked earlier about how active listening isn't a skill many of us have developed to a high level. Often, when we're listening, we're not seeking deep comprehension; instead, we're looking for an excuse to stop paying attention.

In the late-nineteenth century, a physicist, Helmholz, described a process he called "free energy," which measured the amount of work required for states to change in a thermodynamic process. Renowned theoretical neuroscientist Karl Friston uses this theory to explain what happens in the brain when we process sensory inputs.

Think of the brain as the most environmentally conscious person—to the point of being a bit annoying—following you around the house, switching off lights, and unplugging the microwave. We're always trying to save energy by using mental shortcuts and heuristics—and you'll notice that the most common and the most efficient response to new information is a negative. The default position is "*Nope.*"

Neuroscience tells us that one of the key functions of our brains is to make predictions about what's about to happen so we can be ready to act accordingly. The other function is to manage the body's energy consumption. Processing new information, learning, and thinking about complex ideas takes more energy. The relationship between experience, sensory input, genetics, the nervous system, and physiological processes, as well as the impact of our environment and the other living beings around us, is vastly more complex than we yet fully understand. When we think about *how we think*, we're always using simplification and stories to explain ourselves to ourselves. I know that seems circular but it's important, and it contains a clue: we can't control all the variables affecting how our pitch is received, but we can use what we know to give ourselves the best chance of success. We'll talk much more about simplification and storytelling later.

The brain only makes up 2 percent of our body's mass, but it takes roughly 20 percent of our energy to function. That requires more fuel, and in times when food was scarce and future supplies were unpredictable—which was the state of play for the majority of human existence—using up precious calories to process new information itself could be a threat to survival. Thinking meant using energy that could be hard to replenish and could mean not having enough left in the tank the next time a sabre-toothed tiger appeared.

Our brains make predictions based on stimuli, using memories and sense data to decide what we need to do next. These decisions happen at lightning speed and without any conscious effort on our part. The wild part is that the prediction our brains have made then shapes our perception of the next sounds, sights, and other sensations, and depending on the model we've constructed to make sense of the world in that split second, we may be more or less receptive to new information.

This is called the negativity bias, and it's thought to be related to activity in the amygdala. When the negativity bias is in effect, our bodies are pumping with cortisol and adrenaline, which increase arousal and attention, resulting in a stronger emotional response to negative stimuli. This heightened emotional response also helps to ensure that the individual remembers and pays attention to negative information—this is helpful if we need to run away and never come back, but obviously, this fear state is not conducive to hearing your pitch.

The brain pays more attention to negative information than positive inputs and is more likely to code new inputs as a threat. And if it's not a threat, the next step is to discard it as irrelevant. That old evolutionary adaptation helped our ancestors survive by keeping them alert to predators and not using too much energy by processing complicated things we might not need.

When we get our audience talking, asking questions, and considering the idea, they use a more effortful mode of cognitive processing. Rather than a reliance on the intuitive, educated guess mode, we are in the zone: analytical, rational, making memories, and processing more deeply.

How do you get there? It needs to be planned out; those moments when your audience is going to talk should be meticulously built into your presentation. You need to leave a big space for it, set expectations around it, and build it into your time.

If you've got a twenty-minute slot to have that conversation, to do your keynote or to make that pitch, start by planning for a ten-minute presentation and ten minutes of conversation. And I acknowledge that might seem different from any plan for presenting you've heard before, where you plan your content for the full amount of time you have available and then reluctantly open to questions from the floor, but I'd like you to give it a try. I've seen the difference it makes.

We'll discuss knowing when to stop in Chapters 19 and 24. For now, here are my tips to get a strong two-way conversation happening in the first place.

The Two-Minute Rule

My rule of thumb is to set a goal and plan out your presentation accordingly to get your audience talking within the first two minutes. There are solid reasons for this. It's scientifically proven that you are analysing when you are listening, sitting back in the audience receiving information. Your brain is busy judging.

Not only is it judging and assessing, but as Nobel Prize–

winning psychologist Daniel Kahneman says, "The brain is a machine for jumping to conclusions," and generally speaking, those conclusions are equivalent to swiping left on a dating app. Next!

I recommend letting people know as soon as possible that this is a participatory meeting. A great way to do this is by saying, "I would like some feedback, and I'd like it to happen while we're in this room together," backing this energy up with eye contact and body language. This is setting your expectations and outlining the rules of the game for this session. People in the audience know and respond immediately. You see this in their body language: they lean forward and pay attention.

That's just human nature. You put people on notice by getting them to talk up front and early. And at that point, they are engaged and thinking about your presentation as something they're involved in. Often in presentations, there is a sense in which the audience believes on some level that they can be a passenger, bobbing along with the content, and the default position is that they're never truly engaged.

The Opener

You do a small, brief introduction; then you ask a provocative, attention-getting open question; then you wait for answers. And if no one's answering, you let them know: "Okay, I'm not moving on until I hear from three people. This is important, and I'd like to have a conversation with you this morning."

You absolutely wait for those responses. And then, based on what you hear, you can start the introductions, your pitch, or whatever it may be, in the context of this response; you weave it right into your live, unique, never-to-be-repeated presentation.

And from there, you find other moments in your presentation where you make points. And then you call for feedback, a response. Ask something like, "Have you experienced this in your life?" I recommend brainstorming a long list of open-ended questions to keep in your back pocket.

Here is another golden rule: don't ask questions you don't care about the answers to. We do this all the time: "How was your weekend? Did you see that episode of that TV show?" and what we're doing here, in our reasonable and genuine desire for human connection, is wasting each other's precious time.

Plan the Moments

When you're setting out your content and planning the flow, look for three to five moments throughout your presentation where you can see the opportunity for an important conversation. Build in these moments in your content and your delivery so you're getting great feedback, robust interludes of talking, and lots of interaction from your audience. And again, you don't move on until you get the response level that you have planned for.

You then need to rehearse the way that's going to work. And then you need to commit to it when you present it. If you've planned in five moments for the audience to talk, make sure you get that interaction: be enthusiastic, positive, and passionate about it.

If you set this expectation at the beginning and stick to it, the audience will know that is what is expected of them, and they will play ball. If you make it clear that there's no wriggling out of it, and that it will benefit everyone in the room, they will come to the party.

Again, you use things like eye contact and body language to let them know that you're for real—but that it's collaborative rather than scary—when you tell them, "I'd like to hear three responses before we move on because I know that your input is going to make this concept much richer and more effective."

Five to One

I call this the five-to-one rule. For every five minutes of you talking, you need to have at least one minute of back-and-forth conversation. Your presentation will be far more engaging, and people will remember you and your content. They may not even quite know why, but it'll be because they were part of it. You moved them out of the top brain into the midbrain, making emotional decisions, having ownership over the content, and buying in.

It's critical to plan it out. And, even more crucially, to plan for the unknown.

The Sound of Silence

Rehearsing, in general, is covered in depth in Chapter 14, but I want to share a few quick notes in this context because practising these moments is super important. I can't recommend role-playing enough. Get people that you know and trust and ask them to help your pitch by being your rehearsal audience. Ask them to play a range of different roles and adopt different personalities to help you prepare; run through different scenarios so you can plan how to get your audience talking in the presentation, no matter how they respond.

The first role you ask them to play could be passive resistance. You call for comment during your pitch, and your role-playing audience gives you crickets; they give you nothing to work with. Ask them to stare fixedly at the ground; refuse to engage with you; stare at their phones while sighing heavily and rolling their eyes like teenagers. Play it for extremes because, although these things are unlikely to happen, you need to rehearse that worst-case scenario. You need to know what you're going to do in the live moment if that happens.

Then, on another run-through of your pitch, try a different setup: get them to role-play having too much to say. Play out a scenario with so much derailing, distracting chat during your presentation that you lose your train of thought. This is your chance to experiment with how you respond. You can then pull out one of those responses in the live moment.

My advice is simple: never shut down the chatter. You want people talking and in that mental state, but you can't allow people to distract you. You need to think of simple methods to appreciate, acknowledge, and validate their conversation, but curtail it, put a pin in it, and come back to it later.

The best way to get nimble and prepared for situations like this comes down to a technique called Tight Loose. We'll go deeper into that in Chapter 13. But for now, think of this as a way of giving people free rein to say whatever they want, giving them permission and the feeling they can talk for as long as they want. Try to find clever strategies for containing people in a way where they still feel acknowledged and heard, but you stay on track. It's your role to ensure that neither you nor the audience gets distracted, no matter how interesting the comments might be.

Parking Station

Park Station is an oldy but a goody. This is where you create an area in the room or on a whiteboard where you can "park" these interesting but irrelevant conversations.

How you respond is important in keeping the engagement level high from that person and the others in the room. Your response to their suggestions needs to let them know that their input is welcome, and that you are curious and interested, but at the same time, you need to maintain the momentum. Saying something like, "This is a great conversation, but we don't have time to do it justice today. Let's put it on a Post-it note in the parking station. I will follow up with you on this point later this week."

Your message needs to be almost a redirection: "Right now, we need to focus on the presentation because there's so much to get through, and I want us to get to the end together because your time is important, and we can talk about this item later."

Remind them (and yourself) that this is a rare moment that we're spending together. It's certainly not a clipped "Thank you, but we don't have time for this," or any kind of shutdown. Take care to avoid sending the message—

subliminally or consciously—to everybody else in the room that you don't want to hear from them. It can be a delicate balance.

You need to make people feel like they are invited to be involved in a live conversation. And, through careful management and the structure you create, you are nudging people toward contributing to the conversation in specific moments while keeping the moment organic and live.

It sounds almost contradictory: I'm obsessed with rehearsing, but I'm also obsessed with creating an experience that feels like I haven't rehearsed! Both are true.

We've discussed the main reason to get them talking; it's a brilliant way to keep the audience present and involved and help make sure your information is being processed in the forebrain—but if you're nervous, the other benefits are priceless.

If you're feeling anxious, this is your secret weapon. Share the talking work with your audience and you'll immediately feel less pressure. Asking questions also gives you time to compose yourself and plan your next point.

It's a technique that helps me if I ever get worried about the dreaded stutter surfacing. I get the audience to do some or lots of talking for me.

In the space when the audience is taking a few moments to consider and while they're answering the question, you can do a few box-breathing exercises—even nine seconds of box breaths can help you move out of your parasympathetic nervous reaction and calm down. While you're doing this, check in with your audience using eye contact, and plan your next piece of content to adapt to the direction the presentation is moving in.

I'd like to share a story that I think shows you how powerful this technique can be, and happily, I come out of this one looking cooler than my usual examples.

I had to give the best-man speech for a mate of mine. The tricky thing was, I only found out the evening before when the actual best man missed his international flight.

People talk about "imposter syndrome"—well, in this scenario I literally was an imposter. The groom and I were mates, but I was not his best mate by any means; we were business friends. To make matters worse, he was a well-known businessman—the wedding was three hundred strong! It was a big day for him, of course, but the stakes were high for me too; there were people in that room I didn't want to disappoint—contacts, clients, and potential clients.

I was nervous about messing this moment up, not only for the groom but also for myself. I had to pull together the best-man speech about a guy I didn't know all that well and then give it in front of the business elite and their friends.

After some consideration, my approach became clear: I would make it a two-way conversation. Rather than writing a speech, which takes weeks if you're aiming for high quality, I spent my limited time developing twenty provocative, insightful, and funny questions. A much easier task. I know this is unconventional for a traditional best-man speech, but when you've got the mic, you get to choose! I designed a twenty-minute Q&A, and I gave myself the host role.

Preparing my questions in advance meant the pressure was mostly off me in the moment. Instead, the pressure was transferred to the audience. My method was simple: I started the speech with a big open question and then paused. I imagine most people thought it was a rhetorical question, and

I was eventually going to continue with my speech. Instead, I waited a while and then called for answers from the audience. The audience was amused and surprised from that moment onwards. After a few good answers, I then went to my next question. I responded to the audience's answers and added my own colour along the way. It all flowed naturally. As the questions kept coming, so did the energy of the audience. The warmth and humour in the room were special.

The side benefit was that everyone was able to get involved and contribute to this important moment for the bride and groom. To this day, I still have people reminding me of that speech. Most say it felt live and unexpected.

The lesson here is simple: if you can get your audience talking, they will feel more involved and rewarded. As the presenter, you can demonstrate your personality when you respond to what they have to say.

Let's recap: Getting people talking in your presentation is critical to help them stay focused and make them feel involved and invested before you're even at the point of making your ask. To achieve this, you've got to plan for it, build it into your presentation; think about how to get people talking up front and early.

You've then got to rehearse those moments. And then, when you're presenting, it's time to commit.

Plan, rehearse, and stick to it.

If you do that, you will get people talking. You will get people more engaged, and they will find you and your presentation more memorable.

Chapter 8

CREATING CHEMISTRY

"Chemistry can be a good and bad thing. Chemistry is good when you make love with it. Chemistry is bad when you make crack with it."

—Adam Sandler

A key element of likeability is to have chemistry between you and the audience.

We're all familiar with the term but what does it mean and how does it play into public speaking?

Chemistry can be hard to put your finger on and is something that we often think of as there by chance, but I want to show you that it is possible to intentionally create that feeling of chemistry.

In real terms, and according to social science, having chemistry with others involves a connection, along with a somewhat elusive vibe that we feel extends beyond us and the moment. We can look at it as an extra special connection. Chemistry in this context involves how you connect with your audience and, if you are presenting with others, how you and your team connect with each other.

Chemistry might seem more abstract than other concepts we discuss in this book. It also incorporates many other elements from other chapters. But it's important to single out because it's often overlooked, left to chance— yet getting it right can determine whether you win your room or not.

The techniques I'll outline are some methods you can easily apply to create and demonstrate chemistry between you and the audience and you and your co-presenters. They are all reasonably simple to put into practice, but you'll immediately see a shift in your connections and the chemistry in the room.

1. Break the Ice
2. Taking Names
3. Make the Dream Work

$$***$$

While we tend to think of chemistry as something almost magical and indefinable, research shows that chemistry is a tangible phenomenon that arises between people, where the interaction "is something more than the sum of their separate contributions."[23] According to the Interpersonal Chemistry Model, chemistry requires actual, in-person interactions—it's one of the reasons why online dating often falls flat.

When we talk about two people who have "chemistry" together, we most immediately think of shared intimacy and connection, usually in small settings, where you are personally engaging with the other person. There's an excitement in being together, with heightened empathy, passion, attention, and a connection that rises above your average interpersonal interaction. These connections lead to friendships, marriages, business partnerships, and so many other aspects of life we hold dear.

From a psychological perspective, a big part of creating chemistry lies in shared objectives or goals, along with "synchronous" behaviours and a sense of mutual understanding, warmth, and support. It arises from our interactions—and crucially, when we think about how to create or boost chemistry, it's an active and embodied occurrence, meaning that eye contact, body language, and mirroring of gestures and facial expressions can all contribute to creating this alchemical state of being.

Looking at chemistry in an entertainment context is helpful in understanding the power and scale of what we are

23   Reis, H. T., Regan, A., & Lyubomirsky, S. (2022). Interpersonal Chemistry: What Is It, How Does It Emerge, and How Does It Operate? *Perspectives on Psychological Science, 17*(2), 530–558.

talking about here. Because talent aside, the ability to create chemistry with thousands, if not millions, is often the X factor between being a star and not.

Think about your favourite musician or band. Chances are, you've never met them, but I bet you feel a connection with them as if each song was written for you personally. While objectively, you know that's impossible, you can't help but get the feeling that they are relatable and likeable, and that they understand you, and you, them.

For me, that memory is of Freddie Mercury performing at those sold-out mega stadium gigs of the 1980s. A tiny figure in a gigantic auditorium engages the crowd with eye contact; he stares down the camera to connect with those watching at home and encourages crowd participation at every stage. Despite being famously shy off stage, as a performer, he delivered mesmerising shows where his magnetic personality and delivery created a connection with everyone watching him.

Freddie is a great example of both "being" charismatic and "doing" charisma, bringing that energy to audience interactions to make them unforgettable.

I am conscious of how old my reference is and how much my age is now showing! Feel free to insert recent musical examples—people like Harry Styles, Billie Eilish, and The Kid Laroi do this skilfully, too.

Few of us are as charismatic as these superstars, and such flamboyance is impossible to fake (and probably not appropriate for your next job interview or keynote speech), but this is the kind of chemistry a great public speaker aims for with their audience.

The importance of chemistry extends well beyond entertainment. It is also incredibly important in a business context and can make or break a deal, partnership, or even an entire business.

As I write this book, I've been in advertising for more than two decades, and pitching for new business has been a major part of my work life. In adland, securing new business is the lifeblood of any agency.

It's a hyper-competitive, winner-takes-all situation and the possible gains can be huge. Winning a flagship client can be the making of an agency, while losing a client pitch can mean losing staff and sometimes even sounds like a death knell for the agency itself. Pitching costs an agency a lot of money—you're pulling your best people off their regular projects and workloads into the pitch, trying to learn as much as you can about the business but with limited access to the decision-makers, and racing against the clock because pitch deadlines can be tight.

An interesting player in this process is the pitch doctor. Pitch doctors are consultants who mediate between agencies and clients, although they work for the client, and their role is to assemble a shortlist of potential agencies for that client. A pitch doctor would consult with the client and select a group of agencies that they agree are most appropriate for the job. And then those agencies go into a shootout for the work, pitching against each other. And after a few rounds, one agency wins the business.

Pitch doctors spend their days sitting in pitches, and they work with clients on which agency to select. As you'd imagine, they have a good feel for why people buy and why people select one agency over a bunch of other agencies.

Until I spent time with pitch doctors, I thought it would be things like the quality of ideas, price, and content of the presentation. It should come down to these merits, right?

I learned from talking to pitch doctors that, yes, you have got to have good ideas, you've got to have a competitive price, you've got to have a good strategy, and you've got to have good content in the presentation. You need to have all of this, but these are the brilliant basics, the minimum requirements, or a prerequisite—not the deciding factor. Usually, the thing that pushed one agency over the line and lifted one agency to stand out from the rest came down to chemistry. It's that powerful.

My understanding of this power of chemistry in a business context intensified and cemented when I received detailed feedback directly from a potential new client. In short, they thought my agency was too expensive. They liked our competitors' ideas more than ours. They even questioned if we understood their business thoroughly enough, and despite all of this, they were awarding us their multimillion-dollar account. The reason was simple: they liked us as people. That was the exact feedback we received. Our brilliant basics weren't even as strong as the competitions', but we won it anyway based on good chemistry. At the time, this win was a game-changer for my growing agency.

I'm always looking for ways to improve and ways to succeed, so the question then became...what on earth did we do to be so likeable, and how could we replicate it? What was the magic formula?

In our specific case, it came down to the following:

We asked great questions and cared about the answers. We made it personal, so the client felt it was more than just business for us—they could see that we wouldn't be phoning it in. We would bring our A-game to this project.

We demonstrated our internal chemistry. That gave the client real insight into our interpersonal dynamics; they were able to see and feel what it would be like to work with us.

We unashamedly demonstrated our passion. They could tell it was far more than a job—it was an obsession. That's contagious.

We also said no and held our ground when it was worth doing so. Standing up for what you think is right, unpopular or not, is you demonstrating your commitment to your role as an impartial, trusted advisor...not a kiss-arse!

I'm not suggesting you say no just to be controversial, but being willing to say something unpopular when you truly back yourself gives you some edge, creating attention and focus, which can create a compelling energy in a presentation. It's unexpected and charismatic.

All of this shouldn't be overly surprising as it comes back to human nature. We want to work with people we like. So, we instinctively know chemistry is super important. But think about it...how much time do you spend thinking about building and maintaining chemistry when you pitch, when you present? I would imagine not that much.

Unfortunately, most people assume that things like chemistry are spontaneous and come down to luck in the room. And yes, there's an element of that. Sometimes the chemistry between people is serendipitous, but in terms of "doing" chemistry, you *can* plan it out.

Pray to God, but row away from the rocks, as Hunter S. Thompson said.

You can put yourself in a position where you're more likely to take advantage of some lucky chemistry in the room.

You are trying to create a sense of likeability, trust, and relatability that produces a situation where the audience is responding to you emotionally, not just rationally—they want to hear what you have to say; they trust it. They will even defend you to others.

Below are some more tangible ideas you can incorporate into your presentation or pitch plan that will help you do charisma and be charismatic whether it's happening serendipitously or not.

Break the Ice (Without Small Talk)

A strategically and contextually relevant icebreaker is often the perfect way to begin your pitch or presentation.

Don't wait until you're delivering a speech to begin building chemistry. For example, you're about to present at TEDx. Before your talk, you should be reaching out to the organisers to see how you can help with the event promotion. Volunteer for interviews, promote via your social channels and generally build connections with the people who matter.

But as we discussed in our first section, we need to build these connections and forge these links without resorting to small talk. You don't need me to remind you, but I will, just in case: do not confuse this with small talk—the icebreaker needs to be more strategic than discussing your weekend hobbies, the weather, etc.

Small talk is named as such as it is usually deliberately vague, bland, and uncontroversial. It reveals little and can be a distraction from what you're attempting to communicate. Rename it in your mind as "petty talk" or "trivial talk" if you know you tend to drift into doing this. When you catch yourself doing it, ask yourself if you're saying or doing anything of consequence. And if not—stop doing it! Stay focused on what you're trying to say while remaining polite and responsive.

An effective and strategic icebreaker will touch on some common ground between you and the audience, often with a mild dose of self-deprecation. Reach for those universal experiences.

Don't avoid vulnerability or getting real. For example, as everyone has felt embarrassment and feelings of inadequacy at some point, starting with a story in which you're the butt of the joke shows the crowd that you're on their level, empathetic, and capable of laughing at yourself.

Like the icebreaker, stories of personal setbacks and uncomfortable situations scattered throughout your speech can help increase your relatability and further demonstrate that you're no different from the people you're talking to.

We all learn from mistakes, and sometimes the journey to the revelation is as essential as the revelation itself. Again, your chosen story or example here has still got to be strategic—something that is relevant to your overarching presentation and message.

I want to give you some examples to show you what I mean.

If your pitch is about brake pads (think *Tommy Boy*),

do some chemistry work around the way people feel about safety and the importance of brakes in people's lives. Try to make it emotional and tap into those individuals' feelings, but stay on topic.

If your pitch is about dog food, your icebreaker could be, "What if you had to be a dog for a day? What breed would you be in the dog world? What one thing would you love to do as a dog?" Something that's fun and silly but still on topic is one way of getting people to smile and loosen up whilst subliminally asserting your authority and expertise, rather than diluting it. By pulling people into an imaginary world, you've taken charge of their experience. It's charismatic leadership: you're inviting your audience to come and play, demonstrating humility, and creating safety for everyone in the room to contribute.

If you're on a first date—and remember, this counts as a public speaking opportunity—try using an icebreaker aligned with your objectives for the date. Is this someone you could fall in love with? Ask a question that creates intimacy and helps you get to know this person. Remember the thirty-six questions and eye contact experiment we talked about earlier? You could use one of those questions—designed by social scientists in a lab to help couples create intimacy.

Ask, "Is there something you've dreamed of doing for a long time? Why haven't you done it?" Or make three factual "we" statements each. For instance, "We are both in this room feeling '____.'"

By asking and answering these slightly unorthodox first-date questions, you're setting up an expectation that you want to get deep that you're confident in disclosing stories, experiences, and feelings, a key factor in building intimacy and creating chemistry.

Taking Names

Another practical way to build chemistry is to call people by their names. It sounds basic, but it's one of the most effective ways to create that instant connection. What better way to demonstrate that I care about you as an individual rather than one of a roomful of people than by referring to you by your name?

There's evidence that when we hear our name, not only do we instantly pay close attention, but the part of the brain that kicks in is the frontal cortex—the highest cognitive functioning part that we want to always try to nudge our audience's brains toward.[24] It's where we derive our sense of self from—our highest-functioning, most reflective and curious brain state.

Simple, right?

Try to get to know the people in the room and their names. Do the research if you can, and then use their names when you make points. This works more easily if it's a small audience. If it's a medium audience, it's a little more work but still straightforward. You can even do it in a large audience but limit yourself to people who make themselves known to you.

A simple technique I learned from a colleague a few years ago involves drawing and labelling the room. The first thing to do is sketch the table or the area that everyone's sitting

---

24   Dennis P. Carmody, Michael Lewis. "Brain Activation When Hearing One's Own and Others' Names." *Brain Research.* 2006. pubmed.ncbi.nlm.nih. gov/16959226.

in. And then, as people walk in and introduce themselves, you write their name in the position where they're sitting in the room or around the table. Before you know it, you've got a visual map of the people in the room. If you get into the habit of doing this, you will be one of those people who seem to remember everybody's name.

Make the Dream Work

There is chemistry between you and your audience, and then between you and your team, and then between your team and the audience. From my experience, some people, though not many, think about the chemistry between themselves and their audience. But almost everyone forgets about the chemistry between them and their team.

This tip is to get you to focus on the latter and cultivate chemistry between you and your team so that your team is charismatic as a group when presenting.

Presentations often involve teamwork and collaboration, with multiple people speaking in one presentation. It's not all about you. You might find relief in this, that the attention is not all on you, but at the same time, it means you need to account for even more dynamics.

All those years of pitching regularly, and spending lots of time with pitch doctors, has taught me that chemistry between you and your team is super important. It's a big part of why people buy, because they think you, as a collective, are more likeable. If you're getting along in a room, you probably are getting along when you're not in the room. You probably did have fun putting together this presentation.

You're respectful and generous with each other as well as with your audience, and that shows that you're going to be fun to work with. You probably had fun putting together this presentation. And it's human nature. People want to work with people they like.

A critical way to cement that chemistry between you is to rehearse as a team, so your group feels like a well-oiled machine; you know what the next person will say. Practice seamless handoffs and beautiful high balls between people (we'll discuss this in the next chapter).

You don't quite want to get to that old married couple thing where you finish each other's sentences, but you do want that air of comfort and ease, and that will also reinforce your confidence as a collective.

Your ability to be charming and use humour in a self-deprecating way will be boosted by that team energy. It gives you a fearlessness where you know that if you stumble, someone you trust has got your back and can step in to help.

To cultivate chemistry with your audience, focus on enhancing each moment of connection—not just between you and your audience but with you and your team. Use these simple techniques to reinforce positive interpersonal dynamics. Make sure you use the names of the audience if you can, use your teammates' names when you speak to and about each other, make eye contact with one another, and exhibit great body language. As an individual or as a group, you'll be more likeable and attractive to buy from.

Chapter 9

THROWING HIGH BALLS

"If you want to find the secrets of the universe, think in terms of energy, frequency, and vibration."
—Nikola Tesla

Throwing high balls is a key part of how we "do" likeability, how we demonstrate chemistry. It's about how we set out to cultivate collective energy. I know you might think this is all a bit woo-woo, and I do get it—it took me a while to get my head around energy and how to use it in a room.

Throwing high balls is about controlling and sharing energy with intention, particularly in group presentations. It's invaluable for keeping your audience engaged. Energy may seem intangible, but it's conveyed through words, body language, and interaction.

Bringing a focus to how you use and transfer energy in the room can significantly impact how likeable you are to the audience, boost camaraderie amongst your team, and make your presentations memorable.

This chapter is short and punchy and gives three road-tested techniques you can implement immediately.

1. Set the Scene
2. Pass the Baton
3. Ask the Audience

Hippies, reiki practitioners, and old-timey American fire-and-brimstone preachers from the Deep South will all claim that you can do some wild stuff transferring energy from person to person. Interestingly, the scientific community is shifting its stance on how energy works. The field of bioenergy as a discipline in Western science is evolving. Traditional Chinese medicine has been around for over three thousand years and is based on the idea that qi, or life force, is a vital component of the makeup of human beings. It's hard to quantify, but we don't yet fully understand it—perhaps by the time you're reading this we'll have a better idea.

In any case, you don't need to pick a team on this one, but staying open and being curious is generally a great place to start if you're trying to learn.

We've all had the experience of hanging out with someone who leaves us feeling drained—or the experience of working with someone who gives us a boost. Which situation do you prefer? When we love something, we say, "It gives me life"—we mean it makes us feel invigorated, energised, pumped up. In the same way, when you are pitching, presenting, or simply communicating with anyone, an energy exchange happens. But the difference here is that I want you to approach it with awareness and a clear objective about how that energy is going to flow.

As the presenter or communicator, you automatically start with the energy—you start in a place where you control the energy in the room. All eyes are on you in the first instance.

Whether you keep that control is up to you and the audience.

Until now, much of what we have focused on is you as an individual when presenting, but throwing high balls is particularly important when presenting in a group. As Ray Dalio said, "Great collaboration feels like playing jazz." This chapter is about jazz!

For this chapter's purposes, imagine that it's you and a couple of other people presenting together. This is one context in which throwing high balls is important. The other area is where you are getting the audience involved in your presentation, which, if you've read the chapter prior, you know how I feel about that.

So, what does it mean to play ball with energy? Well, it's about you as the presenter, starting with the energy and then throwing a high ball, or a high level of energy, to the person who will speak next, whether that be an audience member, a teammate, or a friend you're presenting with.

Whether you're pitching with your business partner or going to parent-teacher night with your partner, it's about giving the other person or people a great start to run on to when it's their turn to speak.

Yes, it's about energy, but it's expressed in a material way: through your words, body language, and how you interact with the people around you.

Set the Scene

When presenting with other people, make sure you set the scene for those presenting after you. At the end of your section, you have status in the room. Some call it "local star power." You've been in control of the room, and people are buying into you and your content. This is your opportunity to transfer some of this power to your teammate.

As you end your part, say a few words about the next presenter that makes them feel relevant to the subject matter and audience. And do it in a way that cultivates energy and enthusiasm.

For example, "Anna is about to take us through how this idea comes to life. She's had huge experience with ideas like this and recently executed the brilliant XYZ idea that you've probably seen in the news. Anna, thanks for being with us today."

It's simple to do, and with a rehearsal or two, it can feel authentic.

Pass the Baton

Imagine any handover or transition in your presentation as though you're passing a ball of energy to the next person. You need to make it easy to catch.

When you hand over to the next presenter, you can reflect some of your light onto them to help them shine before they've even uttered a word.

Try having one presenter begin a story, then the next person picks up where they left off, creating a continuous narrative woven together by multiple voices. We'll discuss the art and science of storytelling in Chapter 18.

I'm always surprised by the number of presenters I see in the executive world who do their part of the presentation, and then stop dead.

It creates a tricky start for the next person but more importantly, it wastes hard-earned status and power!

I assume it's because they've been so focused on getting to the end of their bit that they've got nothing left in the tank for their partner. I've watched with dismay as the next presenter has their work cut out to bring the energy back up, to reinflate a flat balloon in front of a live audience.

It's disruptive to the flow, it's miserly, and it doesn't reflect well on the team. Would you want to hang out with someone you'd just watched leave their colleague twisting in the wind, let alone hire them to work with you?

This is that "doing" chemistry component we talked

about earlier. This is how you give the audience that little glimpse into what it would be like to work with you and your team. If you show them a strong sense of loyalty, care for one another, and camaraderie, it's infectious, magnetic, and incredibly memorable.

Ask the Audience

Involving your audience in your handovers can be engaging. It also helps you avoid in-jokes or an exclusive feeling between you and your presentation partners that leaves the audience out in the cold.

Think of the newlywed couple taking the dance floor for the first dance at a wedding: everyone's watching and enjoying the good vibes, knowing they're all about to join them in the dance.

When you do handovers, there should always be a genuine invitation to connect.

Try having one presenter ask a question to the audience, and the next presenter steps forward and answers it, using pacing and pausing to build a moment of tension and anticipation.

Another way to invite your audience in is to have two people work together to present a section, passing the mic back and forth for different parts. Along the way, the non-presenter can involve the audience and even ask questions from the perspective of the audience.

You might have ideas about other ways to do this— great! As long as you remember, how you interact with your audience and your team when transferring the focus from one person to the next says volumes about how likeable you are and solidifies the chemistry in the room.

Keep that energy level high, and you (and your grateful team) will be off to a flying start.

Chapter 10

THE IMPORTANCE OF HUMOUR

"Before you marry a person you should first make them use a computer with slow internet to see who they really are."

—Will Ferrell

Using humour is a great way to be human in front of your audience. But let's be clear, in the context of public speaking, humour is not just about telling jokes or being funny. It's about being relatable, showing empathy, and connecting with others on a human level. It's about having the ability to read a situation and know when to use humour to build a connection, to build and then deliberately break the tension.

It can make a speaker more relatable and empathetic and show that you can connect with others. The power of humour lies in the universal, the way humour can narrow divides between us, and its capacity to demonstrate various attributes of effective public speaking like confidence, vulnerability, and influence.

I'll set out some theories about how humour works, different types of humour and explain why I'd recommend avoiding some types and steering toward others. Some forms, particularly self-deprecation, create a strong connection with an audience, paradoxically help you maintain control of the room, and enhance your charisma and likability.

These techniques will guide you to some practical approaches to strategically using humour when public speaking.

1. Common Enemy
2. Ever Noticed...?
3. The Art of the Self-Roast

You can use humour to be self-deprecating; to be vulnerable; to shake up expectations and conventions; to demonstrate that you're open; to show that this will be a fun and energetic meeting, pitch, or presentation.

Humour has a levelling effect. It narrows the divide (whether this is real or perceived) between you as the presenter and your audience. When you use humour, you invite them to come in and have fun with you. As you would imagine, funny people are seen as more charismatic and likeable.

Using humour does several things that are super relevant to most of the attributes of the CLAIM model at once.

It demonstrates confidence: walking into a high-stakes meeting full of senior people you need to impress and cracking wise is quite a power move. It's a little risky, showing confidence but opening you up to failure, so it's simultaneously vulnerable. Humour comes from universal experiences, so you're showing empathy. When you make yourself the butt of the joke, you're being humble and authentic. Humour can take control of the situation, play with undercurrents, and shift people's state of mind, which is highly influential. We are more likely to remember situations that created a moment of emotional intensity—especially if they made us laugh—so you're hitting the memorability factor too.

It's telling that social scientists don't have a dominant theory about how humour works or why we rely on it. We do know that humour exists in some form in every social group on the planet, that there are recorded jokes going back through millennia, and that other species (chimpanzees and even rats) also seem to have laughter and jokes, making it highly likely that humour has an evolutionary benefit, even if we don't fully understand what it is. We know humour contributes to well-being and social cohesion: laughter reduces blood pressure, increases tolerance to pain, and has hundreds of other benefits; laughter helps us to bond with friends and cements sexual attraction.

What's fascinating is that humour changes considerably from one culture to the next. The only universally consistent forms of humour found in every culture (and in apes), are playfighting and tickling, but I would urge you to stay well away from doing either of these things in a work context.

Research tells us that people who are seen as funny are believed to be more intelligent. There are some intriguing studies into the differences between genders. Men and women generally both rate humour as equally desirable when looking for a partner, but many studies historically concluded that (heterosexual) men want someone to laugh at their jokes rather than someone to make them laugh. More recent studies point to the cultural context in which women were deterred, through social pressure, from being funny or "performing" funniness.

From a neuroscience perspective, there are thought to be two "types" of humour: spontaneous and social laughter, called Duchenne and non-Duchenne, respectively,[25] which affect the brain in markedly different ways.

Non-Duchenne is polite or social humour; it's deliberate and intentional. It includes the "I mean no harm" display of smiling that people use to show they're not a threat or the obligatory half-hearted tittering at your boss's feeble joke.

Duchenne humour activates a different part of the

25   Yevgen Bogodistov, Florian Dost. "Proximity Begins with a Smile, But Which One? Associating Non-duchenne Smiles with Higher Psychological Distance." *Frontiers in Psychology*. Aug 2017.

brain, the limbic system, rather than the prefrontal cortex: it's spontaneous, contagious, and irrepressible. A Duchenne smile or laugh is the one you can't help but respond to, the type of humour that lights up someone's face and sets off some involuntary reaction that magically leaves us wearing a face-cracking grin or guffawing in the church, whether we like it or not.

Freud (another guy whom we might have cancelled if he'd been kicking around today) thought humour's function was to release otherwise unbearable tension.

> "Freud's theory was that a joke opens a window and all those bats and bogeymen fly out and you get a marvellous feeling of relief and elation. The trouble with Freud is that he never had to play the old Glasgow Empire on a Saturday night after Rangers and Celtic had both lost."
>
> —Ken Dodd

It's been my experience that the judicious use of humour in a pitch setting allows you to shift the energy, hold it for a moment until it gets almost too tense, and then allow a huge collective sigh of relief when you drop the punchline and everyone can laugh together, creating a strong connection between you, the presenter, and the audience. It's powerful.

A useful way of thinking about humour for our purposes is Benign Violation Theory,[26] which says that humour happens when a person realises two things at the same time: that a norm has been breached and that the breach is benign.

---

26   A. Peter McGraw, Caleb Warren. "Benign Violations: Making Immoral Behavior Funny." *Psychological Science*. Aug 2010.

Humour comes when our sense of how the world is supposed to work is ruptured—but at the same time, we realise this jarring change is not truly a threat because it's a temporary shift. Because we weren't heavily invested in the way things were or because the new model feels safe or acceptable. Here's a terrible—classic Australian—dad joke to show you what I mean:

A dog walks into Bunnings and says, "I want a job."

The guy behind the counter says, "Crikey, a talking dog?! You should be in the circus."

The dog says, "What the hell would the circus want with a plumber?"

Our worldview gets jolted when the dog opens his snout and starts chatting—but we're happy with the new reality where the exasperated dog is just trying to get a job in his chosen calling. It messes with our belief system but in a delightful way.

The kind of humour that works at work gets narrow, and Benign Violation Theory is not a bad framework for sense-checking that risqué gag before you drop it in front of the assembled C-suite in the boardroom of your next pitch. Aussie comic genius Hannah Gadsby cites one of the guiding principles of her comedy as "punching up"—targeting those who are in privileged or powerful positions or the institutions of power themselves.

To put this in a work context, a joke at the boss's expense would breach a norm by disrupting the hierarchical behaviours and expectations of most businesses but does no real harm because that person is in a position of strength.

However, piling on the intern wouldn't be okay because

that person is already at the bottom of the workplace food chain and making them the butt of a joke could do some damage to their self-esteem, prospects in the company, or feeling of psychological safety. And while the CEO could fire you or tell you to get the hell out of the building, the intern has no comeback.

I'm obviously not recommending you sledge the head honcho, unless you have cast-iron certainty that they would welcome this and you have a strong personal relationship. That is a high-risk strategy.

Picking on the intern—as well as being mean, bullying-adjacent, and not funny—is also far from any of the attributes we want to demonstrate.

Common Enemy

The job of humour in a presentation setting is to be inclusive rather than exclusive—you want to bring people together, not drive them apart. One way to do this is to find a common enemy. An obvious way to do this when you're presenting to a company is to pick its nearest rival. Everyone in that room has a key competitor they spend a lot of time thinking about winning against. You'll immediately connect and build some common ground around this shared antipathy—but I want to caution you not to lay it on too thick. It's a small world, and the odds are that someone in that room used to work there (or is about to take a job there); what goes around tends to come around. And my other concern is that it doesn't reflect well on you.

It's a little like when you spend time with a gossipy or

negative person who discloses all sorts of deeply personal information about a third party, whom you're reasonably sure wouldn't be delighted to have all this scuttlebutt about them broadcast around town. And after you shut it down, as you're walking away feeling a bit grubby, your abiding feeling is, "What do they say about me behind my back?"

Ever Noticed How...?

If you're confident that you're unusually perceptive and know you have a talent for jokes, you could try the Seinfeld approach. This option is much safer, pulling focus back to the universal experience and using gentle observational comedy as a social glue.

Jerry Seinfeld described his comedy as "little explorations: my comedy is in the cracks. I talk about the fascination of moments in between the ones that people talk about."

The risk here is of course that "universal" is a highly subjective idea; your jokes just don't land, or the balance between threat and safety comes down too far on the side of "meh," and instead of a witty leader working the room, you come across as intensely boring and out of touch.

"Have you ever noticed the way the numbers in the car park..." you say, as your audience (who don't have a corporate car spot and have probably never even been in the car park!) glaze over and shut down.

The Art of the Self-Roast

For these reasons, self-deprecating humour is your best bet.

Gently mocking yourself is strategic, it's effective, and it works wonders for your general likeability. It shows you're humble and not putting yourself above other people, but by inviting the audience to join you in laughing with and at you, you're demonstrating Teflon-coated confidence.

As to how far you want to go with this, well, you must know your audience and, as you're reading the room, you'll be calibrating and adjusting for the individual's appetite.

You must understand your target audience and pay close attention to their reactions.

But there's no better target for you to choose because you're giving everyone permission to join you in laughing about yourself.

I can't stress enough, though: do not underbus yourself. It's a real tendency I've noticed, especially with people who are just finding their public speaking feet, to savagely eviscerate themselves to get some laughs and build some coherence in the room.

Again, it's a balance: you're not afraid to poke some fun at yourself, inviting the audience into that playful space where your self-deprecating jokes can dial up the tension, release the safety valve of laughter, and get everyone feeling as though we're all on the same side.

But do not sacrifice your expert status and credibility for the sake of a throwaway gag.

In this scenario, you need to maintain your role as the conductor: yes, you can make yourself the fall guy for a moment, but never forget you're in charge of this room, of how long and how far the jokes go, how many lines to put out, and when to reel the audience back in; and it's your call to make when it's time to shift the tone and move back to the subject at hand.

As the theorist Danielle Russell says when writing about self-deprecation in stand-up comedy, "The surrender of power is an illusion."[27] It's a magician moment, and if you get the balance right, it cements how positively your audience feels about you while reinforcing your position as the focus of their attention.

Humour is a hotwire to creating chemistry. And it's also a level of demonstrating mastery. If you think about clowns in a circus performance, when they're up on the tightrope acting the fool, they have to be so proficient at it that they look as though they're about to plummet to the ground while staying in total control.

The importance of using humour doesn't mean that everyone needs to be laughing hysterically or joking around the whole time. Think about where you might be able to inject humour, and which moments you can plan to lighten the mood. Just like when you're shifting the tone, it's another technique in your toolkit to deliver a live, authentic, engaging experience in the room, and it comes down to your good judgment and ability to read the audience as to when and how to deploy it.

Give yourself room to be funny and humorous and have fun. Let's face it—people want to buy from and work with people they like.

---

27   Danielle Russell. "Self-deprecatory Humour and the Female Comic: Self-destruction or Comedic Construction?" *thirdspace: a Journal of feminist theory and culture.* 2002. journals.lib.sfu.ca/index.php/thirdspace/article/view/d_russell.

Humour is a truly amazing way to bump up your likeability, engage with your audience, and move everyone into that playful mode we crave but seldom get to inhabit at work.

Chapter 11

BE GENEROUS

"Attention is the rarest and purest
form of generosity."
—Simone Adolphine Weil

Generosity is something that I talk about a lot when I work with public speakers and craft pitches in the corporate world. And that's because, as the person leading the pitch, you can set the tone and mood and define the context within which this pitch will happen.

Next time you're about to walk into a room, ask yourself, "What mood do I want to create today?" and "How do I want to show up?" Ask yourself and see what pops into your head. Spoiler alert, the right answer should almost always be generous.

In this chapter, I'll explain why generosity is so important and some techniques to create a generous mood in the room. A speaker who can focus on serving their audience, offering valuable content, and enhancing the audience's understanding wins more than the room. The pitch becomes a mutually beneficial experience where both the speaker and the audience gain, rather than a zero-sum scenario.

These approaches will help you present in as generous a way as possible.

1. Adding Value
2. Reciprocity
3. Game Theory

Generosity is a state of mind that can be so helpful in getting rid of nerves in a presentation. The instant you frame this interaction as less about you and more about what you can give others, the attention (and ruthless, noisy self-critique) melts.

Generosity is an attribute thought to have held an evolutionary purpose and given us an advantage over millennia. We are more than the sum of our parts, and the human impulse to share freely and abundantly, often putting others' needs before our own, might be one of the reasons we've survived. You're here because you had generous ancestors.

There is an interesting relationship between giving to others and our quality of life. Social scientists call it reciprocal altruism because, although altruism generally means to give without expectation of directly benefiting, on some level we know that offering help to someone else means we've got some funds in the favours bank.

Altruism is prosocial behaviour. As much as we live in a world where social ties aren't as fixed and vital as they once were, we're still running the same operating systems as humans used 60,000 years ago. The evidence is in our language—in parts of Britain and the US, people say "much obliged" interchangeably with "thank you." In Portuguese, the word for "thank you" is *obrigado*, which comes from the same linguistic root as the Latin word *obligare*, meaning to be tied to, to be liable for, to owe a debt. These connections and interdependencies are how we've evolved and thrived.

I mention this because it reminds us that our greatest potential has always been in our social groups' connectedness, cooperation, and interdependencies. We can go far alone, but we go further together.

The way you view generosity—is it enlightened self-interest, karma, or being the change you want to see in the world?—comes down to your worldview, but no matter how you look at it, approaching a meeting with this idea of being of service moves the needle positively for the speaker and the audience.

I've observed this in my pitches, and I've seen this come to life with all the people I work with; ultimately, if you're thinking about being generous whilst you're making points, when you're offering your ideas and expertise, well, you'll give people more than they need. And you'll take the time to guide them and help them through your content.

If you set out with this as a secondary objective (your first one is always winning the room, of course), rather than getting preoccupied with things like, "How many slides do I need to make this point?" you'll be thinking, "How could I make my content feel generous, feel abundant?" but equally, you'll look upon your relationship with your audience as though you're a guide; you're here to help them and be of service.

It's an unfashionable term, "service," carrying all those old notions of class divides and indentured servants waiting on people hand and foot. But if you consider that offering your expertise to others, in service of your passion, is—thanks to neuroscience—understood to be one of the ways to live a happier life, well, who's doing whom the favour?

Through fMRI technology, we now know that acts of giving and altruism activate the same parts of the brain, particularly the ventral tegmental area, that are stimulated by eating and having sex. This area is linked to dopamine release. We are hardwired to feel good about doing good things for others; our brain rewards us for doing these things by giving us feel-good hormones.

If you approach your presentation with this attitude of generosity, and you see your role as a guide, or as being in service to your conversation partner or audience, then, rather than thinking about the pitch as you convincing them to buy your idea, instead, you're trying to help them figure it out. How can you help remove the barriers between where they are now and the understanding that you need them to get to? You could think about this in terms of servant leadership, a philosophy from organisational psychology that rests on the belief that the servant-leader's primary goal is the well-being, empowerment, and growth of those s/he is tasked with leading. Or another way to think about this is the paradox of the flight attendant. On the surface, the flight attendant's job is to serve refreshments and ensure the comfort of the passengers. But in reality, they're in charge of the safety of everyone on the plane. There's a tension in this dynamic I invite you to explore: how can you take control of the room while being of service?

Adding Value

When people ask you questions, you will look upon this as an opportunity to give as much value as possible.

By doing this in a generous, altruistic, selfless way, you're creating a different relationship. People want to buy from generous people; it's easier to trust someone generous. It helps you move out of the scarcity mindset. I'm not on a guru trip and this isn't a self-help book, but most of us were raised with the idea that there isn't enough (money, partners, jobs) to go around, and often even that we are not good enough. Shifting out of that belief is healthy on a personal level, but I'm here to tell you it's also goddamn effective in a commercial context.

If someone's feeling selfish and projecting anxiety that they don't have enough, it creates the opposite energy to that idea of abundance.

People feel uneasy about working with someone like that because it's like there's an ulterior motive; they are communicating something that's not a million miles away from desperation. That can feel like the presenter is trying too hard; it undermines confidence and trust.

It can feel quite needy if you don't have that overarching framing of your pitch as an act of generosity. This comes through even in the way that you use your body and your facial expressions. However polished you feel you are, your micro-expressions—those tiny involuntary tells that last for less than a millisecond[28] but can be detected almost unconsciously by others—can reveal a lack of ease and comfort that our audience will pick up on, even unconsciously, and lead to a sense of disconnection we know is anathema in the room.

If you've got this idea of generosity foremost in your mind, your expressions will be open, honest, caring, and kind. Your body language will be open. You'll be reaching out to people, seeking to understand what they need and offering them something. And that's what it comes down to. When you pitch, present, or even go into a conversation, you should think, "How can I add value? How can I give my audience the thing that will help them come on this journey with me?"

I acknowledge that this may seem counterintuitive

---

28 Xun-bing Shen, Qi Wu, and Xiao-lan Fu. "Effects of the duration of expressions on the recognition of microexpressions." *Journal of Zhejiang University. Science B.* Mar 2012.

because you're going into these meetings or presentations with a goal. You do want something: you want the client to sign on the bottom line; you want them to change something; you want them to understand your ideas; you want them to buy into your philosophy. That's all fine and reasonable—it's part of the outcome. But if you go into that meeting with a sense of generosity, you're much more likely to get the outcome you want, because people will respond to you if what you offer them is of high value and you aren't coming across as miserly, guarding your expertise like Smaug in a suit.

Reciprocity

As I've been writing this book, I've been posting on social media and giving a lot of my methodology away for free. At first, I was worried that I'd run out of ideas, or I'd run out of things to give away and people wouldn't want more. But I have found it's been the opposite.

The more I give away, the more I have, the more ideas are sparked and, surprisingly, the more I give away to people, the more they want. And it's been somewhat reciprocal: I've gained some insight into the questions people, outside of my usual clients, might have about public speaking, and that's helped me hone and craft this book.

I urge you to think about this notion of generosity. I know I promised not to get too philosophical, but I think this goes well beyond public speaking. If you can front up every day of your life thinking, "How can I be generous today? How can I be kind and come from a place of abundance?" you're more likely to get what you want. That's certainly been my experience, personally and professionally.

Game Theory

You may have heard of something called Game Theory. I was first exposed to it when I lived in New York in my twenties by a dear friend of mine, Dr. Horace "Woody" Brock. Woody is what I call a "big brain" and is somewhat of a global expert in Game Theory. He did his best to dumb it down for me! If you're interested in economic theorems and dirty jokes, then I highly recommend his book *American Gridlock: Why the Right and Left Are Both Wrong, Commonsense 101 Solutions to the Economic Crises*.

To summarise: in any negotiation or pitch moment, two sides are looking at a big, beautiful pie. And in the pitch or negotiation, someone will get more of the pie than the other. According to Game Theory, the person who wants it least often walks away with the most. And from what most of us would see as a moral perspective, it shouldn't be like that: the person who wants and needs the pie the most, the one who's starving, should get the most pie.

But human nature—especially in business—means things usually play out so that the person who needs it the most gets the least. And often, the person who comes from the most, the one who already has the greatest resources, ends up getting the biggest slice of the pie because they're willing to take nothing to get more. They're willing to walk away because they have the mentality that there will always be more pie.

This isn't quite the same spirit as generosity, but it's

adjacent, more along the lines of enlightened self-interest, and it might appeal to those of you who are leaning out and thinking that you came here to learn how to win the room, not to get all sentimental about the greater good.

Whether you think there's infinite pie and you'll get enough of it, or you think that your purpose is to be of service, the approach you need to take is the same.

When you go into a presentation with the idea that you've got enough, you will find that you're happily giving away as much as possible to this audience.

The belief that you've got plenty—and some to spare—sets you up for success in such a way that, nine times out of ten, you end up walking away with more—and so does your audience.

It's a genuine win-win. You both get more out of it, and a nice bonus is that it's just a lot more fun for everyone in the room. I also think human nature is such that people will open up to you more if you come from a generous place.

Rather than the attitude that you need to win and someone else needs to lose, generosity helps you get to a place that's mutually beneficial.

Everyone gets to eat the pie, no one leaves hungry, and the pie is delicious!

Authentic

SECTION III

Get on the same frequency,
think about desired emotions,
and share your true energy.
Yes, I'm talking about a business meeting.

We talked about finding the voice that's most authentically you in the first section. Now I want to get a bit deeper into the idea of authenticity—without getting too life-coach-y on you.

Authenticity has become one of the most overused, loosely defined words of recent times. "Be yourself," self-help books and gurus tell us. This might be controversial, but I think a lot of this advice is wildly irresponsible.

Hugh McLeod is also right on the money— "Authenticity is the new bullshit."

The truth is that the majority of us need to be the version of ourselves that is compatible with paying our mortgages and getting through life with a minimal amount of friction and stress—which is a lot less catchy as a tagline.

Most of us need and use some level of filter. I know I do.

You could argue that the version of yourself when you've just stumbled out of bed, pre-caffeine and with no artificial props like a hairbrush or clean undies is the most authentically, unadulterated you, but I think we all know that will not fly on your next date or meeting. Sure, your BO might be a natural, authentic part of your body, but no one wants to deal with sitting next to your non-deodorised self in the office.

Drawing on some of Dr. Brené Brown's work, being authentic means not pretending to be someone you're not. It means being courageous, but also being vulnerable and embracing your imperfections. And I think this last part, the idea that trying too hard is inauthentic, is what trips a lot of people up when it comes to presenting.

One of the main stumbling blocks I encounter when I'm teaching people how to become great public speakers is the prevailing idea that somehow the best method is to wing it.

It is baffling to me that, in any other area of life, business execs and leaders would, without question, prepare, learn, practice, and apply intense effort to achieve excellence. But for some reason, when it comes to pitching, we have a counterintuitive belief that spontaneity wins the room.

"I shoot from the hip," people say. "I'm best if I just improvise." And then, eventually, they call me, because for reasons that should be starting to be obvious to you by now, standing up in front of a live audience in a high-stakes meeting and flying by the seat of your pants... Well, you know what they say about planning to fail.

I believe that we have a strange blind spot around this idea: we conflate winging it with authenticity. And there are some obvious foundations for this belief. If you think about the most meaningful and magical moments in your life, they probably have this one thing in common: they were entirely unplanned. For me, I think about the day I met my wife. I wasn't looking for love; quite the reverse. We were both a long way from home, in circumstances that were far from how I might have imagined finding the love of my life. But we met, and I knew within seconds that I would marry her. Profound, life-changing, and completely unplanned.

But think about the last incredible gig or spellbinding performance that you saw. What sets the good apart from the great is how a talented performer makes the experience feel like a one-off made just for you. There's a magic, a chemistry between performer and audience that feels authentic and unfakeable. In reality, it's anything but spontaneous—it's meticulously practised and polished, but, to the crowd, the experience feels like a once-in-a-lifetime moment, as raw and unrepeatable as falling in love.

While rationally, we know that the artist didn't just saunter on stage without ever having practised their repertoire, there's something about the live-ness of the event that we somehow believe should translate to how you conduct a presentation. Perhaps because we've seen those emotional wedding speeches where the speaker delivers a beautiful tribute entirely off the cuff, leaving everyone in tears. Perhaps because we fear that the audience will trust us less if we seem to have practised, we will seem less authentic.

The fact is that just isn't the case and shifting our point of view from our experience to that of the audience can be helpful here. I feel strongly about this: you are not being less honest and authentic if you rehearse.

Like all the key concepts in this book, there is some nuance between being authentic and *doing* authenticity. Expressing authenticity means vulnerability, but I want to be clear about this: taking a bigger risk by extemporising doesn't make you more courageous and therefore more authentic.

The impromptu, unrehearsed approach does not translate to how things land for an audience in a work context or any situation where the crowd isn't enthusiastically on your side from the outset. And even big stars performing to their most hardcore fans can have nights when something is off; the crowd picks up on a moment of weakness and can turn on the performer.

Actors, musicians, and comedians talk about "dying on stage." When you're riding the wave of everything working perfectly in a live environment, it can be the most exhilarating experience in the world, but when it goes south, and your audience becomes hostile…it can feel physically agonising. Quite frankly, I don't know why you'd want to put yourself— or your audience—through this misery.

If we go back to the key elements of authenticity and the component of vulnerability and bravery, let's reframe our notion that setting ourselves up to fail is more real and authentic.

Vulnerability means being aware of your shortcomings and the areas in which you do not perform at your best and bravely working to overcome them. There is an inherent vulnerability in asking other people to spend time listening to you present: you don't need to create an artificial veneer of vulnerability by doing this badly.

We wouldn't believe an elite athlete was being fake by training for a competition. It's about doing what you can to remove the obstacles that hold you back from being your best.

In my opinion, there isn't much that's more vulnerable than taking an idea you believe in passionately, want to see come to life, and standing in a room full of people you need to persuade to get on board with your pitch.

We tend to think of authenticity as a twenty-first-century preoccupation. The ancient Greeks were obsessed with this idea too. 2,500 years ago, great thinkers and speakers like Euripides and Plato discussed the importance of standing up in public and fearlessly telling the truth. The word *parrhesia*[29] doesn't have an exact translation in English, but it carries the meaning of speaking courageously and without fear, and— fitting with our modern ideas about vulnerability—despite

---

29 *Parrhesiazesthai* translates roughly to "to say everything" from *pan* (everything) and *rhema* (that which is said).

the risk to the speaker.

The concept of parrhesia wasn't only about being fearless; the word has connotations of the outward expression aligning with your fundamental values and beliefs as a person. Telling people what you truly and deeply believe can make us feel extremely exposed and incredibly freeing.

In those days, the dangers of speaking your mind could be enormous. Socrates, for example, was condemned to die for the ideas he shared—but even today, we still need to overcome our fears and stand up bravely for ideas we think are worthwhile.

Returning to the collective's power again—when we share an idea we think is important or big or will create change in some way, we're also inviting others to join us in making the idea better. The idea doesn't have to be perfect: however well-thought-through your pitch is, the second you share it with others, you're asking for feedback, builds, and modifications—and hopefully, the idea will emerge stronger and become more indelible as a result.

We want to set ourselves up for success, to give our big idea—which is an authentic expression of who we are and what we believe—the best chance of connecting with our audience. We want the audience to have the experience and magic of us being live, responding to them as though we are fully present. This one-time-only bespoke performance demonstrates our human vulnerability and builds trust.

It won't be long before an AI can write a speech, based on every speech any human has ever recorded, that will rival the work of the most compelling orators in human history.

What makes the difference is the magic of unrehearsed,

live human interaction.

In a world of endless replication, live is becoming more and more important, and presenting well is the differentiator.

Often, a combination of nerves, pressure, and a lack of preparation makes it hard to be your best natural self. I've certainly seen hundreds of public speakers who are authentic and confident in who they are and what they stand for when you talk to them one-on-one. But a strange thing happens when they start talking in a meeting, they take the microphone on a stage, or they're being interviewed by the media. They suddenly become inauthentic—they come across like they're acting or playing a part, trying to be someone or something they're not.

Well, that's one of the quickest ways to lose your audience and become annoying and forgettable. That's what we will work on in this section. These techniques are for you to think about and to grab and use immediately: five thoroughly road-tested techniques that will help you demonstrate your authentic self at your best.

And a quick side note: you will probably have heard people extolling the virtues of having a shot of whisky, or using substances before you present, in the belief that being a little disinhibited will help you be more relaxed and come across as your best self. In vino veritas and all that.

I've certainly seen plenty of people in advertising taking that approach back in the day, although I'd say it's a lot less prevalent now. Putting aside any moral perspective and the likelihood that you risk getting fired if you get caught getting high in most workplaces these days, I don't think this is a good strategy.

I'm sharing techniques, not cheats, and I'm sorry (not sorry) to say I don't think you can use shortcuts to become a great public speaker. Booze or a bump might give you that temporary false confidence, but it's a fine line between that and bravado, and what tends to happen is the boost fades as you go, leaving you less sharp, even sloppy. You can't tune in and read the room or think on your feet, and one tricky question can leave you floundering. And it's also not sustainable. If you're pitching every week and rely on artificial means to get you through, you'll end up with a serious dependence fast.

I want you to get to a place where you're buzzing from your interactions with the audience and the energy you create when you're winning the room...and chemicals will only get in the way of that feeling.

Being authentically yourself and delivering ideas you believe in, live and direct to an audience who might just want what you're offering could be one of your most positive experiences. I remember the first time I experienced that feeling.

In my career's early days, I worked on the M&M Mars business at BBDO. My team had a big presentation in the infamous fishbowl at the Mars HQ in Hackettstown, New Jersey. The fishbowl was a large conference room in the middle of their open-plan office, and it was made entirely of glass, floor to ceiling. Everyone in the company could see you present at the meeting. There was nowhere to hide. This was my first fishbowl presentation, and it was to the CEO.

I was still a junior back then and had a minor role in the presentation. That might sound manageable to you, but I had to stand up and speak in front of a lot of people more senior and knowledgeable than me—people whose inclination would be to be impatient and less tolerant of me and any mistake I might make, people who could make or break my fledgling career. Don't forget I was still figuring out how to manage my stutter, let alone how to hold attention and take command of a pitch situation.

Often a small role in a presentation can be more daunting. It's hard to make an impact with a small amount of content and time, but easy to instantly feel like the weakest link! My overwhelming fear was that I would be seen as the stupidest person in the room. But I had rehearsed the hell out of my little part and felt ready to deliver. My boss opened the presentation. As usual, he was supremely good, and he had the client eating out of his hand. He wrapped up his section, paused, and then handed it over to me.

As I stood up in the middle of this glass amphitheatre, for no reason, I started smiling. It was the weirdest feeling. Here I was, sweating bullets…but smiling.

Then people began to smile back. It was infectious. Even the CEO started to smile. I can't explain precisely why or how it happened, but this presentation suddenly became a game. I was ready to play.

Looking back, I believe it came down partly to my extensive rehearsals, but mainly due to my boss's example. He loved presenting, and it showed. I caught his vibe and ran with it!

I went through my well-rehearsed points but also found time to observe the live moment. I found myself acknowledging the obvious tension in the room and that I was stepping up in this moment…and, more than my fears and the sense that I was being watched like a bug under a microscope by everyone in that building, it felt amusing. A little absurd to see me here. And that sense of slowing down and noticing everything meant it became funnier again, broadening my smile, and the audience's smiles widened in response.

By the end of my section, I didn't want to sit down. I was live, present, and loving it. The energy in the room was great and I felt like I had built a real bridge—my first bridge with a client.

My presentations and pitches changed on that day for good.

In this section, I will outline five vitally important elements that will help you get to that place where you feel comfortable being the authentic version of yourself that the situation requires. Where you're performing at your best, the atmosphere in the room feels live, unique, and bespoke, and you and the audience can get into that flow state together in an exhilarating way.

Chapter 12

READING THE ROOM

"Sometimes you need to be aware of the bigger picture you are missing."

—Derren Brown

Reading the room, like many of the concepts we cover in this book, is not a single-faceted idea and has a little more complexity than you might first imagine. It's about understanding other people's moods, attitudes, and backgrounds. It also involves understanding the context of the room and the audience, monitoring the audience's reactions, and being aware of how you also contribute to the energy of the room and the audience.

Empathy and attunement are the critical skills we need to build to read the room.

We need to pay close attention to our audience and then respond to them by adapting our presentation, shifting gears, using body language, changing our vocal pitch, and so on.

You aren't present to mirror the audience but to serve them. Cast yourself in the role of magician, if you're into archetypes, or the conductor in front of an orchestra.

This chapter will help you understand why you need to be present, self-aware, and adaptable to create positive change and effectively connect with your audience. The techniques are:

1. Leave No One Behind
2. Record Scratch
3. Cue Cards

To read the room usually refers to a real-life roomful of people, but if we apply more expanded definitions to the concepts of *people* and *room*, we see it to mean a certain demographic or clientele. The expression "read the room" is found as early as the 1970s, but in this case, it was used by a professional cat burglar to mean observing where valuables were located in a room and to plot the thief's access to them in the future. In queer ballroom culture of 1980s New York, to "read someone" was to make an exacting analysis of their flaws and then let them know of your appraisal via devastatingly accurate jokes at their expense. The meaning evolved further, and by the 1990s, marketing executives began to use the phrase to mean to understand the motivations, feelings, and moods of a certain group of people. And that's more the vibe I'm going for here. It's about careful analysis, tuning in to even subtle shifts in your audience's body language, eye contact, and mood—not so you can read them to filth but so you can adapt and flex your presentation in response.

When we walk into a room to begin a presentation, we automatically impact our audience, so how we enter that space is highly relevant.

By now, I hope you recognise the fact that decisions are made much earlier in the presentation process than when you get to your final slide—the one with the words "Next steps...?"—and awkwardly raise your head to look at your audience for the first time in your entire pitch. I'm joking, of course; you've come this far, and I know you wouldn't do that to yourself—or your audience.

But knowing that the buying decision is being made on several factors, and our presentation is only one contributing element, we might focus more on reading the room than on our content.

I've watched so many speakers breeze past their audience's clear signals and nonverbal cues, ignoring the flashing neon buying signs, and doggedly continue on with their content, blithely unaware that they've just talked themselves out of a sale.

On the face of it, yes, they're in that room to present their idea, and the client is there to listen and evaluate, so technically they're doing what the situation demands—but, in reality, any human interaction is a lot more nuanced than that. A speaker who acts as though the audience is a roomful of mannequins is unlikely to get to a yes.

And the shifts that can happen when you're paying close attention can be significant; it is not to be underestimated, and again, like many of the skills I discuss, there's a degree to which your job here is to relearn what you've forgotten.

Who would you say are the most attuned people on earth? Who do you imagine are the most insightful and astute when it comes to reading a room, calibrating the feelings, moods, and behaviours of others? If you guessed detectives, teachers, or psychologists, you're in good company because these are typical answers, but you're entirely wrong.

The most attuned humans are babies: their whole existence is about absorbing every available cue from their environment and their caregivers, soaking up information like tiny, adorable sponges and deriving their sense of safety and happiness from the actions and reactions of those around them. Sadly, their lack of clear verbal communication and tendency to scream loudly makes them a bit of a hindrance in a pitch setting—but once again, the point here is to remind yourself that this is a skill you once possessed. Like riding a bike, this will return to you more easily than you imagine when you start practising it.

These are skills that you need to apply differently

depending on your audience. The ability you might have to read a room of only three or four people and the ability to tune in to an audience of a thousand are pretty different—but if you remember my story about crashing and burning after I made small talk at a school conference, those thousand people will give you plenty of signals and information about how your talk is being received, whether you like it or not.

When we think about attunement—and I'll talk more about this in Chapter 15—you want to not only gauge the vibe as you walk into the space but also begin thinking about how you will affect a change. Of course, at this point, you can bring some things out of the Winning the Room toolkit as you develop your skills in shifting the tone, changing gear, etc.

But fundamentally, it starts with an accurate and meticulous assessment of your audience, which you will gain from keen observation. Gauging the mood and receptiveness of your audience to a message is something we all already do to some degree, even if we're not aware of it or not doing it for strategic reasons.

Say I start telling you a joke. As I build to the punchline, I'm monitoring your reactions—eye contact, stable posture, a small smile—these are all encouraging signs that my message is being well received.

Conversely, if you're fidgeting, staring off into the distance, or rolling your eyes, then I will have to change tack if I want my joke to hit the mark.

Something similar happens every time we speak to each other, whether consciously or not. We might not have been keeping this ability nicely honed in a deliberate way, but it is an innate ability that we all have.

Reading the room is about reminding ourselves to put our empathy skills into practice, and then—and this is where we get smart about it—it's about how we apply this skill in tandem with the other skills you're learning to create positive change.

Now that you sense the audience is feeling a certain way, or you're feeling some resistance to an idea, how can you respond, step into the live moment, and connect with them?

The audience is giving you nonverbal cues all the time. Become a student of body language, facial expressions, and tone of voice. These can give you strong clues about how they are feeling and what they are thinking. Look for patterns of behaviour: Notice if certain behaviours or reactions are common among a group of people. This can help you get a sense of the overall mood in the room.

Ask open-ended questions to help you gather more information about how people are feeling; encouraging people to share their thoughts will give you a great deal of insight, not only into the individual's perspective, but also their colleagues' attitudes and state of mind.

Trust your intuition. Reading the room means being attuned not only to your audience but also to yourself. We are in the habit of overriding our instincts, which I would argue is a major waste of a whole chunky dataset. Often, you get a feeling about a situation without any clear sense of where that vibe is coming from—and, if you're honest, I bet you feel confident that these feelings are on the money most of the time. Don't ignore your gut instincts but also make sure you gather enough information before acting or making any decisions. Trust, but verify, as the tech kids say.

However, once we have mastered attuning to our audience and being empathetic, we need to reframe and remind everyone in the room why we're there: to address a challenge or problem they need help solving. It can be helpful to take a 20,000-foot perspective. What's the situation in the room—and what's the bigger picture? We're there in service of the greater good, solving this problem together.

I want to caution you against being so attuned to the audience that it can throw you off the reason you're there. Your purpose in being in the room is to solve a problem collectively, but your role is not simply to reflect the audience's state of mind or being but to shift it, elevate, and change it—as far as you can, strategically. Being attuned will enable you to identify how you need to move the energy and use all the skills you are developing—changing gear, shifting the tone, and creating a vibe. On the flip side, bringing a honed awareness of your own state of mind is vital: we're constantly processing sensory data from external sources and our bodies. We know if we're feeling "off," but we are seldom able to tell exactly why—a shift in blood pressure, being slightly dehydrated, whatever it may be—and our brain will be trying to make sense of this input. Being self-aware and as centred as possible can help us avoid projecting our experience onto others.

Whenever you walk into a room, you will notice that there is already a tone in the room and a mood; everybody is arriving with their baggage—walking in, bringing whatever happened in the last meeting, or the email they just received. Maybe they're coming in thinking about what will happen in the next meeting—or maybe they're thinking about what they'll have for lunch.

And it's your job to read that room and then adjust your introduction and the way you start your presentation to match and contribute to that room. This technique is all about being present, attuned, live. Observing and appraising what is happening in the room with your audience and then reacting and interacting with them while you're public speaking.

Comedians are the gurus of reading the room. Part of what makes a comedian great is their keen eye for human observation. And this translates both to their content and their delivery.

Stand-up comedy is not just about making people laugh; it is about connecting with the audience and reading and responding to their emotions in real-time. This type of incisive emotional intelligence is a rare and valuable skill that comedians develop through years of practice and performing—and in truth, from dying on stage, having their jokes bomb, and all the other dramatic phrases we use to describe the agonising feeling that the crowd is turning on you.

If the audience is not responding well to a comedian's material, a good comic will be able to pick up on this and adjust their performance to bring the mood up. They might tell some more light-hearted jokes or share a personal story to connect with the audience on a deeper level; riskier, but potentially more effective, is to call out the audience, to acknowledge that the jokes aren't landing. Then, as the tension that arises as the audience feels themselves under scrutiny begins to build, the comedian gives the audience an "out" from this awkwardness by cracking a joke. The relief that follows will often translate into a big laugh—but it takes nerves of steel and the confidence that only comes from having done this successfully many times before.

It can be quite tiring—you're "on," every sense on alert and running through your content—but when you get to that live feeling, you get a huge boost of energy from your audience. I'm sure we've all experienced this. When you're presenting, and you're getting information and feedback back from your audience—a smile, a nod, or some level of agreement—you get that endorphin rush. "Wow, my content is connecting, it's working, they understand me."

And as a result, you get confidence and energy from that, just like when you have a great conversation with someone.

First up, you want to be looking at the people you're presenting to. We talk a lot about eye contact in this book, I know. But eye contact is a key component of reading the room. And whilst you're looking around the room and engaging with the people, you're looking for their tells: the things they do that let you know they are into this content or they're not.

Either they like you or they don't. They believe you, or they don't. They want to hear more or they don't. They have a question, or they're not engaged enough to formulate a question.

These are some examples of things you must look for while in the room. And if you see indications of any of those things, you need to address them straightaway. If you see people are uninterested or losing interest in what you're saying, no matter how disruptive this feels, you must stop and check in. You can check in with a pause or a verbal prompt: maybe you'll say something like, "Hey, I just want to check in and make sure this is connecting with you; do you understand what I'm saying? Let me know if any of this isn't clear. I don't want to keep going unless everyone's on board."

Leave No One Behind

When public speaking, I have a rule for myself: I leave nobody behind. I am religious about it. If I notice that I've lost an audience member, I will completely stop my presentation and engage with that one person until I have their attention back. I urge you to try it next time you're presenting. You'll be surprised at how the whole audience responds.

You can use some self-deprecating humour here—"Are you getting something out of this, or were you expecting something else?"

I'm giving you examples of the way I frame these kinds of interactions; my style is informal, and I like to have some banter and keep things causal—until I shift tone and get deep or serious for a moment—but that might not work for you; you need to find questions and check-in moments that are natural and authentic for you.

As we've discussed, we need to clarify that until we hear from the audience, we're not moving on. Interaction and participation are not optional. However you do it, make sure it's open, insistent, and requires a genuine answer. You don't want to check in with an audience in a way where you're nudging them toward telling you what you want to hear so you can carry on regardless. People need to feel they have permission to ask.

Get people to communicate how they're experiencing your presentation alongside you, as we discussed in Get

Them Talking. The way they've responded, and their verbal and nonverbal cues, will give you the information you need to decide where to go from here. Because if they're just thinking it and not communicating that with you, they're not truly engaging. They're not remotely close to being influenced by you, let alone buying from you. They're not giving you their full attention; ultimately, you're wasting your time and theirs.

Record Scratch

If your presentation isn't connecting with your audience, maybe it's time to stop presenting. Sounds defeatist, but I'd prefer to give people time back rather than drone on about content that isn't relevant.

People will learn to expect this from you; in the future, they will turn up to your presentations because they know it will feel bespoke, relevant, and respectful of their time. And if it's not…it'll be over quickly!

Think about any presentation moment as rare and precious. You've got past the EA. The calendars have been aligned. Everybody's finally in the room at the right time. Maybe they've got the budget ready. If you're trying to sell something to someone, don't squander that important and unrepeatable moment.

If you're reading the room and see your content isn't landing, turn the screen off and have a conversation instead. You can amend your slides on your time and send them later but do not waste this opportunity. If you don't read the room, you will leave people disinterested and disengaged. They will just float along in your meeting; they won't bite, buy, or agree.

Maybe there'll be some friendly chit-chat because you know each other, and you've probably done some good chemistry up front, but they won't commit; what you're looking for in any great pitch is commitment, which only happens if you read the room.

There is a vulnerability in saying, "The content isn't working, and I need to take a completely different tack." It might feel disastrous, but you're demonstrating a high level of authenticity and confidence, and it reads as expert-level emotional intelligence.

Cue Cards

You're looking at your audience or conversation partners, their micro-expressions, and what their body language is telling you. This technique is eye contact on steroids; I'd use it sparingly, and it's only effective in smaller groups, but paying attention to eye-accessing cues can give you some incredible feedback to help you refine your presentation and delivery in the moment.

We will talk more about how to craft your pitch to make it memorable in Section V, but remembering that everyone processes information differently can be helpful.

The patterns of eye movement someone uses indicate how they are processing information; if you're noticing a lack of engagement, you can adjust your communication style accordingly.

This isn't just a glance in each direction but a repeated habit of eye tracking. People typically have one dominant method for processing and storing information, and their eyes indicate whether they're locating the information visually, auditorily, or kinaesthetically.

If someone is accessing visual memories, recalling something they've seen in the past, you could prompt them by using visual aids or describing an idea in a highly visual way. Someone who depends on visual constructions or creating a mental image of something new would benefit from being asked to visualise what you've suggested or to describe their vision for the future.

People who use auditory recall, or process by imagining the sound, respond well to storytelling or analogies to help them understand your message. Help auditory memory-makers connect by asking them to recall a similar conversation or experience. Kinaesthetic information types process by imagining a feeling or a physical sensation. You can also glean some cues from the language people use: "I don't feel comfortable," "I look at the problem like this," or "That doesn't sound right." The way someone frames their feedback out loud gives you a good clue as to how they process input and what you need to do to connect with them.

A great rule of thumb is to make sure you share your ideas in a multifaceted way that hits all these processing types—asking people to share something from memory, describing something with a lot of detail, shifting the pitch of your voice, or talking about the content in an emotional way and inviting the audience to do the same.

The more attentive and attuned you are to your audience, the better you can adapt your pitch: being live, responsive, and authentically yourself.

Chapter 13

TIGHT LOOSE

"Most of the time I'm thinking,
I'm glad that scene was improvised."

—Larry David

In simple terms, Tight Loose is about learning your speech Tight, and then presenting it Loose. I'm 50 percent confident that I came up with the idea of Tight Loose, but I am 100 percent positive that all great public speakers the world over are using this technique, most of them unknowingly. It's their process.

But how does one achieve this? While there are many techniques you could employ to increase authenticity, from the practical to the spiritual, Tight Loose is the most powerful one I've come across, because it's easy to enact, and the positive impact happens almost immediately.

Tight Loose is a technique that allows you to cultivate authenticity and achieve a deep connection with your audience. It's a way of preparing for your presentation and a way of being whilst presenting. Of everything in this book, Tight Loose is the most daunting technique to apply. But it's also the most powerful. When people commit to Tight Loose, it is nothing short of transformational.

Czech psychologist Mihaly Csikszentmihalyi identified a process called "flow state"— when the cerebral cortex is working at its full potential, the hundred billion cells in our brains (almost as many as the number of stars in a galaxy) all fire together, carving new neural pathways allowing us to create art, music, ideas, inventions, innovations.

When we are in the flow zone, our work is effortless, we experience complete absorption in the task at hand, and we find our work intensely pleasurable. The more time we spend in flow states, the happier we are. When you're using Tight Loose to its full potential, that's how it feels to present.

Before we get into the technique specifically, let's take

a moment to consider why authenticity is so important in this context. What happens to you, the public speaker, and your audience when you're giving an authentic presentation? As I've said, it's not a presentation but a two-way conversation. Something that feels real, honest, and one-to-one. When a public speaker feels authentic, they are believable, and more importantly, buyable. Whatever they are "selling" is easy to buy.

Think for a moment about the best public speaker you've ever experienced. Someone you were in the room to witness who had you, and likely everyone else, completely enthralled.

I can almost guarantee that a few things were happening during this mesmerising presentation. First up, they had no notes. They appeared to be speaking off the top of their head and freewheeling in front of the audience. They probably also felt live and in the moment—unshackled in a way where they could tailor their content to the occasion and the audience. And finally, it probably felt like you had all the time in the world together, and certainly never looked rushed. There was room for jokes, anecdotes, and a little side story here and there, things that felt off-topic at first, but then they looped it back into their overall message. There's a good chance they were in a flow state. Magic!

I've been in that kind of audience before, several times. I recall the first time vividly. Aside from loving every second of the presentation, a loud voice in my head asked, "How the hell are they doing this?!" and "Why can't I do this?"

Like most acts of magic, they were following a technique.

Authenticity is like holding a small bird in your bare hands. The more you try to secure it, the more likely you are to smother and kill it. But equally, hold it too loosely, and the bird flies away. A delicate balance that needs to be not too tight and not too loose!

I was recently talking about Tight Loose in a boardroom with the leadership team at a luxury fashion house. After I spent a good fifteen minutes unpacking the concept, one of the immaculately dressed executives raised her hand and quipped, "So, Tight Loose is about learning your material?"

She was, for the most part, right. Yes, practising your material is the genre, but Tight Loose is about an outcome rather than just something you do. It's not just about learning your material but about how you use that learning when presenting in the moment. It's a specific technique that ultimately helps any public speaker feel more authentic and better connected with their audience, no matter what curve balls the environment or audience might throw at them.

Sound simple? I hope so. The practical application of this technique gets slightly more complicated and, according to what I hear from most of my clients, bloody terrifying!

Here's how you do it.

Step One: Prepare Your Presentation Tight

Rehearsing your speech is the foundation of Tight Loose. If you don't know how important rehearsing is, please read on. It's an essential practice to learn, and we will undoubtedly dive deep into the subject in this book, particularly in the next chapter. But for now, we'll discuss preparation in the context of Tight Loose.

Learning your content Tight is about practising not only what you'll say but also how you will say it.

To start, write your speech in long form on standard A4 paper. This is the definitive longest-form version of your speech—we're nowhere near the palm-card stage right now.

By long form, I mean not just the speech itself but the speech annotated with notes and descriptions about how you will present it. You need to get detailed at first, thinking about and documenting the specifics, like how you're going to stand, what you'll do with your hands, and precisely when you're going to smile. Thinking through and planning these extra layers is essential at this early stage.

I suggest you create a code in your notes so it's easy for you to follow and remember. Maybe you underline the things you want to emphasise, highlight the moments when you want to make sure you're making eye contact with your audience and add a simple ellipsis when you're planning to pause. The more detail the better; marking up your speech notes is an art.

Once you've got all of this written out, you'll notice two significant things. First, it's long. Second, so much of what you present is not in what you say but in *how* you say it. This is a great thing to realise upfront and early.

Step Two: Rehearse Tight

So, you've got your long-form notes. Now it's time to get Tight.

The process of rehearsing is so important. As mentioned, I've dedicated an entire chapter to it coming up, so I won't go into too much detail here.

If you want to get Tight on your content, you need a minimum of ten rehearsals. Yes, I said ten.

I know, I know, it sounds like a lot. Most people are probably looking up from this book right now, wondering how they'll ever have the time. My response is always the same: if your speech is not worth rehearsing ten times, is it even worth presenting? Maybe it should be an email or a group text. The bottom line is that you can only present something Loose after getting Tight.

Loose Loose is a disaster!

For this part, it's most beneficial to enlist the help of someone you trust. By trust, I mean someone who will tell you the truth and give you honest feedback: good, bad, and ugly. Choose wisely. If that's too daunting, you could just film yourself and give yourself feedback.

Let's say you've enlisted a friend. Start by presenting your content to them. As you present, make sure you talk about what's in the margin. Tell them *how* you will say each point and give it a go. When it's feeling good, start to act out the directions in the margin too. If things aren't working, find a way that does and mark up your notes. This is the driest of run-throughs, so you should feel free to make mistakes, double back, and experiment with things. I recommend doing this a few times through. As you present, write down notes and continue to mark up your speech.

The first two or three times you rehearse, you'll find your speech gets longer, and your notes get more detailed. You'll be thinking that there's now no way you can fit this entire performance into the time you have, but don't worry. This is a great thing. Keep the specifics flowing. The aim here is to get your head around how you're going to present the content.

Then, on about the third or fourth rehearsal, you'll want to start reducing your notes. Maybe you change it from A4 paper to a palm-card style. The last five rehearsals are about reducing your notes, with the objective of eventually having no notes at all.

By the night before your presentation, you've rehearsed more than ten times, you know your content inside out, and more importantly, you know precisely how you will say it. Every word, every gesture, and every pause has been planned out and choreographed. You are a well-oiled public speaking machine, and you're wound tight on this content!

Now, throw away your notes and go to bed. When you wake up, present it Loose.

Step Three: Getting Loose and Letting Your Presentation Flow

This is always challenging to get your head around, and it takes some guts the first few times you do it. And I know from my clients that this can be even more daunting than their usual or old way of presenting.

The key is that you don't look at your notes on the day of your presentation. This is the hardest part. Every time I get to this point in my workshops, I see hands shooting up with questions all over the room.

I get it. The first time you do this, it will feel wrong— reckless even. How the hell are you meant to remember all your content? Here's the thing: you don't have to, and you couldn't even if you tried...and that's a good thing.

You will forget your exact content. But instead, you'll remember the intention of your content. You'll move from presenting bullet points to communicating a feeling.

In a Loose presentation, you can focus on your audience and move through your content with them. It's a live presentation for a reason, and you'll be in that moment with your audience. If they smile and engage, you can smile and engage with them; take a leisurely swim in your points. If they look down or seem confused, you can take your time and check in with them to bring them back on board.

Anyway, back to Tight Loose. Most audiences start off paying attention. They notice your every move. If you turn up loose, they will relax with you and trust you. As your loose presentation unfolds, they will be more and more intrigued with you and your message. It's like a great conversation on a first date. It's surprising, genuine, and 100 percent in the moment.

Your points probably won't come out in the exact order you wrote them. Maybe your points will come out 1, 3, 4, 2, 5. It doesn't matter because only you will know that the order is slightly off. The natural reordering of your points is a brilliant thing for your audience. It feels spontaneous and real. Dare I say it? It feels authentic!

The key is to relax. You've learned your content Tight. You know it back-to-front. Go into the moment with this in mind, and rather than squeezing the bird tightly, loosen your grip a bit and let the bird fly free in your hands.

The first time you practice Tight Loose will be scary. It'll feel like a load of work, and you'll wonder whether it's worth all the angst...right up until you're in the room presenting. This is when you'll feel a shift. That shift starts small, but as you notice yourself relaxing into your content, it builds like a rolling snowball. The further you get into your presentation, the more you realise that you remember your content. You're in control of your content...and your audience. As we discussed in Section I, confidence begets confidence.

Better still, you're not just saying it. You're doing it in your way. You're expressing yourself.

Tight Loose does more than just improve your public speaking ability. It's like a window into a whole new world of public speaking. It's a real penny-drop moment for most of my clients and has life-changing potential beyond public speaking alone.

Tight Loose is addictive. Once you've used this technique successfully, you'll only ever want to use this technique. Anything else suddenly feels rigid, phoned in, and inauthentic.

Chapter 14

REHEARSING

"Practice like you've never won.
Play like you've never lost."

—Michael Jordan

Rehearsing is essential, but how you rehearse makes the most significant difference.

My take on rehearsing is that it only starts when all your content is locked in, you've got a group of people in front of you to rehearse to, and those people are ready to role-play like the actual audience in the way they react, respond, and ask questions. If any of these elements are not in place, then you're not rehearsing—you're just doing a run-through.

Real rehearsing is the difference between good and great, and great and unforgettable. It's essential for even the most polished presenters. That said, carving out the time (and courage) can be difficult.

We will discuss the optimal ways to rehearse and learn a series of techniques.

1. Role-Play
2. Swap Roles
3. Eat the Elephant
4. Add a Rogue
5. Rehearse in the Room
6. Q&A

Effective rehearsal can make or break careers and businesses.

Most people tell me that they don't have time to rehearse. For those who are confident in their abilities, it can be seen as an unnecessary waste of time, while for those lacking confidence, it can be a difficult, uncomfortable chore. Either way, you will not perform optimally without it.

Sporting analogies make the importance of rehearsing

clear, even when you are the best in your game. Take the hundred-meter sprint, which you might assume is the most straightforward sporting event in the world (literally!), especially if you're, say, Usain Bolt. But the reality is anything but. Yes, he's always running in a straight line for the hundred-meter, but there are so many other variables that he rehearses (or trains) for. He will train in the heat if the next event is in Dubai. If it's an outdoor meet, he will ensure he's prepared for the possibility of rain. He will train with the wind in his face, at his back, and from the side. Essentially, he is preparing for any variable that may be thrown his way.

Moving to the more nuanced sport of ballet, the Misty Copeland story is special. From humble beginnings, she became the first African American woman to be named the American Ballet Theatre's principal dancer, despite being told multiple times throughout her childhood that she had the wrong body shape—and the wrong skin colour. How did she do it? Practice and grit. Underlining her determination, even to this day, Misty takes a class or two every day and rehearses for at least seven hours a day in the lead-up to a performance. She doesn't rest on her laurels and knows that practice and rehearsal still matter, even when you've reached the pinnacle of your profession.

Both Bolt and Copeland are masters of their craft. One might assume that their training would be about maintaining fitness and the rest is muscle memory, but that's not the case. They employ consistent, high-quality rehearsals to best prepare themselves for whatever variations are thrown at them and maintain their position at the top of their game.

The same concept is just as relevant for the arts,

and someone who epitomises this was James Brown. The Godfather of Soul was also known as the hardest-working man in show business because, despite being at the top of his game for over half a century, he remained just as committed to rehearsal and driving exacting standards from his band in his last-ever gigs as he had been at the start of his career. Yeah, he had a reputation for being a relentless perfectionist, but he never gave a bad show. He knew that no matter how familiar you are with your routine and your audience, no two shows are the same, and rehearsing will have you prepared for anything.

You might be inclined to dismiss this level of rehearsal as excessive and only relevant to superstars, but if you're reading this book, I've got to think you want to be a superstar in your field. And in the corporate world, the stakes are often even higher. Not to be too dramatic, but one excellent presentation or pitch can reset and make your career, or erode and break your career. Similarly, the success of an entire business can be cemented or shattered in one meeting. This is especially relevant if you're part of a start-up, a product developer, or a creative with a project to sell: even if you don't have a specific invitation to sell your wares, you must be ready to give that elevator pitch any time. These are the kinds of stakes we're dealing with.

The rehearsing process I teach is rigorous. It takes time. And in my opinion, if you don't have time to rehearse, maybe what you're doing is not something that needs to be presented. Perhaps you can just put it in an email, write a document, set it, and send it across. But if you think this is worth presenting, you do think this is worth pitching out loud, then you have to rehearse. It's that simple. And I believe it is a crime not to prioritise this.

When I talk to people about how we will be rehearsing, and setting ourselves up to win the room, and they look panicked or dismissive, I know they're imagining the emails piling up and dealing with the time pressure they're already facing. While I know they believe me when I say it's vital, that they won't succeed without it, they're figuring out if there's a hack or a shortcut. But there are no shortcuts, sorry. You have to do the work.

The only real shortcut you can aim for when it comes to rehearsing is to get so used to the process of rehearsing that it becomes second nature to you—because, when you're in the habit of doing something well, you inevitably end up doing it faster. Developing a strong rehearsal practice now will help you take advantage of opportunities that come up without much notice!

I want to tell you this personal story—another one in which I'm not covering myself with glory, but it illustrates how important it is to be prepared, even for an impromptu pitch! If you have something to sell, you need to rehearse the heck out of your proposition and be ready to hustle whenever you get the opportunity.

It was the mid-2000s, and I had just started my ad agency. I had scheduled a catch-up with a few bankers I knew from another business. These guys were friends of mine, and my understanding was that it was casual; I had no expectation that we'd talk serious business in any formal setting. As I arrived at their office in the big end of town, I noticed my name on the welcome board in reception. This usually only happens for big clients and important pitches. I shrugged it off as a mistake or maybe even a prank by my friends.

The alarm bells should have started sounding when I was greeted in reception and ushered into a large conference room, but I wasn't paying close enough attention and breezed in without a care. To my shock, it was filled with executives. I was expecting two or three people, and now there were at least ten suited and booted senior execs eyeballing me.

I had inadvertently walked into a pitch, which was my rare opportunity to pitch for the bank's advertising account, something I dearly needed at this early stage of my agency. At this point, I should have acknowledged the mix-up and rescheduled, or at least excused myself for ten minutes to collect my thoughts and strategy. I didn't though, thinking that it would still be a friendly audience, and since I knew the two decision-makers well, surely I could still think on my feet and wing it.

I quickly found myself dive-bombing. It was profoundly embarrassing, and I lost a lot of confidence in those thirty minutes—not just about my new venture but also my role in business more broadly. I'd missed the mark and demonstrated that I didn't instinctively know my business well enough to sell my services. I was only a month in and still figuring it out, but that didn't feel like a valid excuse at the time.

Once I returned to the office, I prioritised being ready to pitch at any time. And luckily, I got the chance to go back in. That time, I took some of my team with me. We had rehearsed our offering to within an inch of our lives. We ended up redeeming ourselves and eventually did some work with the bank. But if I had been well-rehearsed from the outset, I wouldn't have relied on luck or relationships.

This makes me think of another recent story. I was flying to Tasmania for a big annual conference I helped organise. It's a high-profile event featuring the best global minds in finance, innovation, and health. Everything was organised, and the team and I were ready to roll until the phone rang.

If you've ever managed events, you'll know they are predictably unpredictable beasts; if you don't have to navigate six crises before breakfast, you start to wonder what's gone wrong that you don't know about yet.

But this was a biggie, even by event standards. Our highly respected regular MC was calling to apologise because he wouldn't be catching his flight; he'd caught COVID-19 instead. We didn't have much time, but every year we have a delegate list of high-powered people; we knew we had a serious media stalwart flying in at any moment. He's a household name, and many would say he was Australia's best interviewer, but he'd retired and was happily out of the game.

He has a reputation for being the biggest brain in the room. As he was boarding his flight to Tasmania, we called to ask him to step in and deliver the MC role. He didn't agree straightaway, but he had the hop, skip, and jump across the Bass Strait to think about it, and when he landed, he agreed to step into the breach.

As the creative director of the conference, I train all the speakers, so I met up with him that evening. I thought it'd be a quick handover and then move on. After all, this guy has been doing far bigger gigs than this for forty years.

To my great surprise, he not only wanted to rehearse, but he also wanted to rework the entire script. Working until midnight, we did five full run-throughs on stage—in the room, working out the angles, the stage, and the AV setup. He worked through the entire running order, over and over, until he was comfortable. He turned up the next day and shot the lights out. A brilliant performance.

This story speaks for itself. It's a great lesson that *everybody must rehearse and prepare, no matter how talented or experienced*. Never rely on your natural (or learned) skills.

To start rehearsing effectively, here's what you need to do.

Know what a rehearsal is and stay disciplined. Reciting lines in your head or in front of a mirror isn't a proper rehearsal (although it can be beneficial). A good rehearsal requires an audience, or at least to be in front of someone who can critique your performance once your content is locked in.

Don't get discouraged if your rehearsals aren't going well. Mistakes in rehearsals are where we learn about our strengths and weaknesses and where we can make adjustments. It's what they're for. And one mistake incurred in a rehearsal will inevitably be a mistake avoided when it's genuinely time to perform.

Role-Play

During rehearsals, ask your audience to role-play and act like your real audience—one person is easily distracted and looking at their phone, another is exhibiting negative body language, another is interrupting with constant questions, etc. Experiment with ways to overcome these curveballs public speaking can throw at you.

You won't get feedback in the room. Rehearsal is your only opportunity to iron out the kinks. Realising you should have completely rethought the order of your content midway through presenting it will make you scramble to adapt, rather than feeling supremely confident that your Tight preparation means you can flow with whatever arises.

Swap Roles

When you're rehearsing with your team, take the opportunity to swap roles. The lead person becomes the support act and vice versa. What do you notice about your section when someone else performs it back to you that needs to change? Practice those transitions and workshop some ways of passing between yourselves with high-energy, high-ball generosity.

Force yourself to change ten things about your presentation.

Eat the Elephant

How do you eat an elephant? One bite at a time. Chunk it down. Dismantle your presentation into sections and rehearse them separately; take them out of order and mess around with the flow.

Add a Rogue

Bring in someone who knows nothing about your content and your ideas. Does your pitch pass the pub test, where you make sure you can get your point across to someone from a different world? What would need to change for you to explain it to your mom or your grandad?

Even though your audience will be, in all probability, experts in the field, the more you can reframe and simplify your ideas, the more transmissible and memorable they become.

Even the most intelligent person needs more neural processing power to decode big words and densely complex descriptions than simple language and explanations. Would you rather have them use up their precious and limited attention, making sure they understood you correctly, or reduce friction, get a positive emotional response, and ultimately be easy to buy?

Experiment with how you present—will you be sitting or standing (or a combination of the two), will you use props, will you use any technology to help convey your message? Try presenting your content seated, and then try presenting while pacing around the room like a caged tiger. How does this shift the tone, and could you incorporate different styles at key moments?

Rehearse in the Room

Call the client and ask if you can rehearse in the room, you'll pitch in. You'd be surprised at how often people say yes to this (and it's another great knowledge-gathering opportunity).

If you're going to present slides, make sure you've got the slides up in rehearsal.

If you're going to use a particular clicker to move through your slides, again, use that clicker.

If it will be in a big room, find a big room to rehearse in.

What will you wear? Plan it out and ensure you wear

that outfit or a similar one when you rehearse.

What you're trying to do is to closely replicate the live event before you do it.

Usain Bolt trains by running the same distance, in the same conditions, in the same shoes, trying to replicate what the live moment will be like—partly so he can improve his performance, and partly because he's carving a neural pathway that says, "I've done this, and it went well, so I'll just do that again."

Q&A

Recognise the importance of Q&A and rehearse for it. When someone is listening to you speak, it's much like someone walking into a shop. They are being analytical in their approach—comparing prices, models, colours, etc. Only when they approach a shop assistant does their analytical approach change, or can be changed, into buying mode. That's what Q&A is about, and it will help you gauge your audience's buy-in to what you're saying.

Perfect being Tight Loose. Right up until the night before your presentation, memorise the content, practice your body language, and rehearse, rehearse, rehearse. Make it tight and systematic. Then, on the day of the presentation, put your notes away and present it loose. If you have adequately prepared, your presentation will appear off the cuff and you can adapt to any circumstances you encounter.

Chapter 15

PUTTING THE AUDIENCE ON NOTICE

"A lot of people never use their initiative because no one told them to."

—Banksy

How you start your presentation is important because your audience judges you from the moment they see you. I'm sorry, but they are. Anyone who says they aren't is lying to you. Maybe you're even lying to yourself. The sooner we face this reality, the better.

This chapter covers the subtle interplay of influence, power, and control at work in a pitch or meeting.

Your job in the first few minutes of any presentation is to signal to your audience that you are in control of yourself. I'll explain some of the tensions behind this and offer some techniques to manage that situation so that you can move on to taking control of your content and the audience.

I've developed these techniques to demonstrate to the audience that you're in charge of this room.

1. Start Strong
2. Switch Up the Status Quo
3. Eyes on the Prize

We're about to go into it in detail, but in short—never underestimate the significance of a strong start, the need to disrupt the dynamic in meetings, and the importance of keeping the objective in your sights.

As you approach your living room to speak to your extended family, a boardroom to break some bad news to your boss, or the TED stage to drop some profound knowledge on the world—you are on!

In those first few moments of your presentation, the audience is waiting to see what you do and say. You haven't even earned it yet; they are still paying attention to you. This is your moment to grab and maintain that attention throughout your presentation.

People are sizing you up in those early moments of a presentation, often subconsciously trying to sense any sign of weakness. They are asking themselves, "Is this person comfortable and in control? Are they worthy of my time and attention? Can I relax into letting them take the lead, or will I need to assert my claim to being in charge?"

Like most things in life, you can frame all of this as a negative or a positive. On the negative side, you can lose your audience before you've even said your first word. People probably won't start throwing tomatoes, but they will tune out. You know, looking down at their phone, thinking about what's for lunch later, or worse, they may get up and walk out to a more important thing they had on that day. These happen daily in business meetings, first dates, and sports team gee-up sessions. But on the positive side—you have their attention, and I urge you to embrace it!

It sounds aggressive, and I guess it is. No bombs are dropped, but a definite struggle for power is going on.

It's why so many of the phrases we use in professional settings draw from the language of conflict. When things are going well, we're "killing it," "smashing it"; we "deploy" a tech platform, "capture" leads, and "target" our customers. Like it or not, for most interactions in business, the perception and pursuit of status are critical. Once you've lost status, it can be almost impossible to reset expectations.

I called my corporate workshops Winning the Room decades ago. I more recently called this book by the same name, because I believe there is a battle going on when we public speak: a struggle for dominance between the presenter and the audience. It's not necessarily audible or aggressive, but it is happening. This is how humans are wired. Yes, we are incredible at collaboration, but that tends to be within a hierarchy. We are naturally competitive animals, and at the start of any interaction—and a presentation is no different— there is a natural jostle for status. Whose moment is this? Who is setting the agenda? Who deserves attention in this room? And more than attention, we want esteem.

Like any good military strategist, you've got to take control early. So, how might you go about this?

Start Strong

First, you need to address your audience with your eyes, facial expressions, and body.

Start with your body. Ensure you enter the room with your body open and facing your audience. Avoid doing anything that feels defensive. Crossing your arms is obvious, but even things like fidgeting, pacing too much, or covering part of your face with your hands will subtly tell people you're not confident and in control.

Try striking the Wonder Woman power pose in the privacy of your home, not in the meeting. Or any power pose you like—head upright, shoulders back, arms outstretched. Please give it a go. I'll be here when you get back.

Did you notice how strong and centred you felt when you stood like that? Think about that energy and what you're projecting outwards. Then dial it back to maintain the feeling of being grounded and in charge, but without walking into a room overtly pretending to be a cartoon superhero. Then think about eye contact and facial expression. As you enter the room, try to catch the eye of a few people in the audience. Spend a moment with each of them. A smile, a nod, basically an acknowledgment that you (and they) are in the right room.

It's that moment just before you start your presentation. It's important not to rush. Resist the urge to fill the space straight away. Instead, take your time. Let silence happen, and smile around the room in that first moment of anticipation.

Take a deep breath through your nose, and then let a long breath out as you say your first words. Send it from the base of your belly to the back of the room.

Fill up the space with your energy and take control of the moment. Observe your audience and ensure you take care of each person with eye contact and a check-in if they're looking distracted.

Switch Up the Status Quo

Small meetings often feel casual and can become conversational quickly (more challenging to get a firm decision). Conversation is great for empathy, chemistry, and the presenter's nerves. However, a conversational meeting is bad because it makes the moment feel like the stakes are low, and it's much easier for the audience to be noncommittal.

How do you ensure your small meeting carries weight and doesn't end up feeling like mates having a chat? To keep a small meeting in the decision-making zone, up the level of drama (significant pauses, eye contact, gear changes). Use unexpected body language—for example, stand up when everyone else is sitting.

Delegate someone to write things down for the group to read, whether on paper or on a whiteboard, signalling that these ideas and thoughts are worth recording.

I said in the last chapter that businesses could be made or broken in one meeting—here's an example of how that looks when it goes well and switching up the status quo was one reason it worked.

My team and I had been appointed as consultants to a tech start-up in the retail space. We had a significant meeting with Australia's biggest retail business bosses. They own the biggest and most prestigious shopping centres in the country.

We were pitching for them to become business partners and to make a multimillion-dollar investment.

We needed to pitch from a place of strength and success. Truth be told, if we didn't get the partnership (and investment), the business would likely run out of money ("runway" in start-up parlance) and fail before it had even gotten off the ground.

While we might know status is always in flux and shifts depending on the context, in a pitch of this nature, with a large, mature, and hierarchical organisation, there's not much space for this kind of nuance. We knew we would have to go in owning the meeting and keep control.

We spent weeks planning out the pitch. We knew we'd only have a limited window to grab attention and get a yes. It needed to be snappy and potent but still with depth and rigour—a tricky balance. We also knew we'd be in a big room, but there would only be five people. There were three of us and two of them.

It's hard to make your pitch or presentation feel big or noteworthy in front of small audiences. While this can create great chemistry, small audiences often end up feeling like low-stakes chats, and that was not the vibe we needed them to feel while we were asking for, quite frankly, a shitload of cash and support.

The tech platform was based on a card analogy, so to bring it to life and imbue the meeting with a feeling of abundance, we created large-scale playing cards. We had these cards beautifully designed and made.

We weren't quite beating our chests like apes, but there was, without question, a decision to use these creative pieces as a display of status. By investing in these gorgeous items that had been created just for this meeting, we were signalling that we were resourced and had plenty and some to spare. If you think back to Game Theory, by showing we could afford to spend money on these impressive props for a single meeting, we were flexing our muscles and demonstrating that we had the courage of our convictions.

We made six points, and we dedicated one large-scale playing card to each point. The tech platform had an interface where the user would swipe through cards. This made the presentation format feel even more relevant and delightful.

On the day, we dealt out the cards in front of the two bosses as we presented. It was fresh, tactile, and intimate. The cards also enabled us to create drama and intrigue as we dealt them out.

That one meeting shaped what became a four-year relationship. Yes, we got the investment: they gave us verbal agreement right there in the room.

But more importantly, that meeting set the tone of the relationship for the next four years. With one meeting, we had positioned ourselves (and the business) as creative, brave people with power in our own right. This was precisely the type of partnership this large and conservative organisation needed!

What is it we're trying to do when we pitch? Simple: get people to make a decision.

Eyes on the Prize

Keep everyone on target and on task. Keep coming back to what we're here to do—figure this out beforehand and have a shorthand way to bring the group back to that purpose/objective.

This is critical, and I would say it's the point of failure for most people. Ask for the money. I'll repeat it. Ask. For. The. Money.

Make sure you know exactly what you want out of the meeting and be prepared to return to that ask—repeatedly if needed. You'll need to develop a callus about this one. Even in a context that is by nature a commercial one, the number of people I've worked with who have a visceral reaction and entrenched reluctance to talk about, let alone ask for, money is astonishing.

There's still a lingering cultural taboo against discussing finances, which often spills into a pitch setting. As though, by asking for sign-off, we will kill the vibe, or it will reflect poorly upon us.

I'll say two things about this: that is the primary purpose

of a commercial meeting, and in a high-stakes situation, nothing robs you of status faster than squeamishness about asking for the decision you came here to get.

And secondly—money is merely a symbolic form of value in our culture. You're doing this presentation because you have a concept you believe is worthwhile; you've brought your best, most authentic self, your entire focus and intention, to this room—if you don't think that makes the ask worthwhile, again, send the deck by email and save everyone some time.

Deepak Chopra said, "Money is life energy that we exchange and use as a result of the service we provide to the universe."

Feel better? Now go and get that yes.

Chapter 16

SETTING THE MORAL

"Fight for the things that you care about,
but do it in a way that will lead others
to join you."
—Ruth Bader Ginsburg

This chapter outlines the importance of setting the moral, why this matters, and how to do so effectively.

I want to stress that when I use the term "setting the moral," I don't mean judging others against a religious or philosophical set of values; it's not a question of morality.

The moral works on a deeper level than facts or figures.

What is the moral or bigger purpose behind your presentation or approach? What unifying idea brings you and your audience into this room?

Setting the moral means bringing your values and aspirations to life through this narrative and gives the audience an easy-to-remember statement about your purpose in this meeting.

The key message or lesson (the moral) should be stated upfront and revisited at the end.

This technique also encourages audiences to recall and retell the speaker's story, making it an effective tool for idea advocacy. This chapter will explain how to set this up and deliver it.

1. Define the Moral
2. State the Moral
3. Moral Pay Off

Any public speaking opportunity is a chance to tell a story. And clever storytelling means setting the moral up front and giving the audience closure that it's been delivered at the end.

Simply put, a moral is a lesson that can be derived from a story or experience. It's the enduring idea you want firmly lodged in the heads and hearts of your audience as they exit the room.

TED Talks are littered with speakers Setting the Moral. You'll notice that at the start of many TED Talks the speaker starts with a big provocative question. Questions like "Can robots be creative?" "How do you know you exist?" and "Would you opt for a life with no pain?" This is the speaker drawing your attention to their speech's deeper meaning. They start here because they want you to think about it for the duration of their speech, while they meander around in the subject matter. Then at the end of their speech, they finally return to that original question. Often their last words on stage are an attempt at an answer.

Setting the right moral is a balancing act. As per the TED Talk examples, you want your morals to be big and bold but equally, you want your morals to ring true in the end. Here are some excellent Setting the Moral examples I've seen work effectively:

"What would happen if we told it like it is?" For a soon-to-be-launched law firm, this helped them think differently about how they could communicate with clients. In a landscape of jargon and over-explanation, how might they cut through with direct and transparent language?"What would the world miss out on if your business didn't exist?" For a major telco business, this got them to consider their impact on their customers and society. Rather than being distracted by their always-on marketing plan, we could focus the client on the areas where they indeed added value to their customers.

"Would you continue to operate if you knew there was a better way?" For a medical technology brand, they could speak to doctors in an arresting way and get them to reconsider the facts they believed.

We will talk more about the role of storytelling in Chapter 18. Still, the reason that setting the moral is in the Authenticity section is that when you stand up in front of your audience and you tell them a story where you set a moral, you are sharing your vision of the world, at least the vision that exists in your story.

By setting the moral, you're giving the audience a clear understanding of who you are and what your story is about at a deeper level. It is one of the most powerful ways I can think of to communicate what's important to you, what you value, and what you believe to be worth working for, allowing them to connect with the authentic you through values, not just content.

Another way to describe the concept of the moral is what Hollywood writers would call "the takeaway message." What's the vision, what's the role we want to play in the world, what do we want to leave our audience with, and what is our collective value proposition for the change we seek to create?

Think of any great film or book, and there is (usually) a three-part structure around one central idea; there is a rhythm and a structure that works with the atavistic parts of our brains. On some deep cellular level, we love it and value it deeply when someone tells us a story that aims to help us make sense of the world.

There is something deeply satisfying to the audience about this structure. It's how human beings have passed on information since the dawn of the species. And that's because the human brain is designed to consume and remember stories. Just like any great story, your pitch needs to have a moral.

This chapter is about setting that moral up front. The first thirty seconds of your opening your mouth should be about setting the moral. Then you can go forth and tell your story throughout your presentation. Toward the end, you revisit the moral you set up front and then fulfil it.

That is the reason, the why, behind your presentation. That is what you're looking for when thinking about the structure of your pitch content.

Define the Moral

First off, you need to figure out what that moral is. But again, it will not be about facts, stats, money, or precisely what you're asking for. Instead, it's about the human intent behind your content or idea. The bigger picture. What does it mean?

Think of the moral as the backbone of a story. It's the organising principle the whole story is built around.

Some morals appear in stories the world over, like "Good always triumphs over evil," "Think before you act," "Work hard and prepare while times are good (so you can survive hard times)," "You're stronger than you know," "Always be true to yourself," "It's never too late," and hundreds more.

Now I'm conscious that they sound like things you'd see in a storybook or a movie. And you're probably wondering how the hell this relates to your pitch. Well, I ask you to search for deeper meaning in your pitch.

If you want to engage with your audience authentically,

you need to hit them on a deeper emotional level, not just on a rational level.

Suppose you find yourself stuck in the **what** (factual, logical, rational); try asking **why**. Why are we showing up to do this? Why does this matter? Why should anyone care? In my creative practice, I ask myself, "Why?" five times.

You will feel it immediately when you strike something emotional and authentic. You need to hunt for that moral in your presentation material. And then you need to set that moral upfront.

State the Moral

Now that you've defined your moral, it's time to state it.

If you want people to engage with your moral, you must clearly say it. As in, say it out loud. Yes, I'm being that literal.

I often see presentations where the moral is buried on a slide or amongst a series of other points.

It's your job to give the moral of your presentation breathing room. Plant it in your audience's head like a seed, and water it throughout your presentation, allowing it to grow and bloom by the end of your presentation.

Simply put, your moral will not land with your audience if you don't say it out loud.

Moral Pay Off

The best time to get the payoff from the moral is at the end of your presentation. This is where you harvest the fruit that grew from the seeds you planted in the introduction piece and nurtured through the presentation.

You need to set that big open question upfront; then, throughout your presentation, you continually come back to it right up to the end when you answer that moral.

During your presentation, you can discuss things related to your moral, but you should hold back the pieces that answer the moral till the end.

To use an analogy from one of the classic stories, just like Hansel and Gretel, you carefully leave a trail of breadcrumbs throughout the presentation; the audience follows that pathway through the content until the final moment, which is one of redemption. In this story, Hansel and Gretel triumph over adversity through their ability to work as a team and their resourcefulness.

When your presentation has a strong moral, your audience gets to see who you are and what you stand for. You give them something bigger to identify with. This type of presentation, or story, is compelling because it invites people to join forces with you in the service of something more significant and rewarding.

Influential

SECTION IV

Figure out how to help your audience connect with the right decision. Hint: it's not about convincing or tricking anyone.

Influence is something you hear a lot about these days. Influencers on social media, influencers in mainstream media, the government, friends trying to influence what we will do next Saturday, your peers, people at work—everyone's trying to influence everybody to do something.

This section is about being influential as a presenter or public speaker. How can you influence your audience to think and act in a different way? There's no objective metric or way to calculate influence; opinions are divided as to how you become influential.

How can you influence others toward your opinion, ideas, or whatever you're trying to convey and communicate to them? Being influential involves cultivating a heady blend of trust, power, and aspiration. Still, if we want to change someone's behaviour or attitude, we also need to get their attention—or better yet, their esteem—and understand how people make decisions.

Now, it's essential to acknowledge that there's a cousin of influence: manipulation. It can seem like a fine line between influence and manipulation. The difference is in the intention and how we go about enacting it.

Influence is about getting people to come toward your idea, to think differently and act differently, because (we believe) it's the right thing to do; because we think it would be beneficial for them (and it's okay if it benefits us too).

Benevolence is one of the critical attributes of influential people: we will take guidance from someone we believe has our best intentions at heart. We generally tend to think of someone as benevolent if they show they care about us—if they're generous if they demonstrate that they are concerned for our interests and well-being (as well as their own).

Manipulation is the dark side, the shadow version of influence. It means taking people to places they don't want to go to and being deceptive about either the end goal or how you're trying to take people there.

It also means trying to change behaviour to benefit the manipulator, which may harm the other person.

Influence contains an overt and explicit statement of intention. We can be upfront about what we want to achieve rather than seeking to change behaviour in an underhand fashion. It's why it's important, for example, that people with a large following on social media disclose that they've been paid to spruik this product or that; because their followers often trust them and have some moral if not legal responsibility to be truthful about their motivations.

When we enter a room, step into a meeting, or even stumble into a cold pitch situation, we have tacit permission to seek to influence the audience; we are undeniably trying to change hearts and minds, but doing so with the knowledge and consent of the other parties. It can be characterised by mutual understanding rather than a power imbalance; we also have a common objective or goal, and considerations of the audience's needs and interests are paramount.

To be influential, to persuade our audience to shift their thinking, to change the way people think, act, and behave means first getting and keeping their attention. We'll talk more about this in Chapter 22, but as a general guide, to grab attention, we need to be novel and surprising; we need to disrupt our audience's expectations and create content full of sensory cues and moves them toward a change or a yes. If there were a formula for influence, it might look something like this:

Likeable/high-status speaker + attention-grabbing content + aligned with heuristics = influence.

This is almost absurdly oversimplified, but thinking about the levers and motivations driving behaviour change is key to being influential.

Understanding that how we present ideas needs to align with how our audience makes decisions can seem like a complicated proposition. It's fair to say that studying cognitive bias and heuristics is probably a lifetime's work.

It's also important to note that we simply can't control all the variables that might shape individual decision-making on any given day. But to be influential means getting our heads around the basic idea that cognitive biases influence decision-making.

Cognitive biases and heuristics, or shortcuts, are patterns of thinking that can (and do) lead us to make irrational or illogical decisions. And understanding what's going on when people are making choices can help us at least try to reduce the friction and stress that decision-making can create in the audience.

Designing our content and how we present it to hit these markers, rather than starting on the back foot, can make a significant difference, and a lot of this is built into the techniques in this book.

For example, tips like "taking control" and "shifting the tone" are about disrupting the status quo in the room before we even begin presenting. That's not in service of a giant ego, but rather, it's strategic and planned to give ourselves the best chance of coming in hot with fresh energy and a higher likelihood of influencing the audience.

Here's why that matters. Anchoring, also known as the anchoring bias or the primacy effect, is the tendency for the audience to rely on their initial impressions when they make choices.

People often anchor their decisions around whatever initial information they receive.

This bias can influence how people interpret or discard new information. It's why first impressions matter so much.

Thinking about this logically, a group walking into a room quietly, then sitting down, politely waiting for the client to invite them to speak, has done nothing to indicate that they're less capable, creative, motivated by success, or any other marker that influences how we make decisions.

The tatty shirt I wear or how I introduce my teammate doesn't have much to do with the critical evaluation of a creative idea, investment opportunity, or the viability of a new product, right? But I am here to tell you that everything about that first impression, the information the audience starts processing as the door opens, sets us up for success or failure.

Walk into that room with low energy, demonstrating low-status behaviours or with a lack of confidence in your body language, and your audience is then automatically comparing whatever happens next, no matter what, to that initial perception. It means our brains are rapidly rejecting all new information in favour of the original prediction, even if that initial anchor point isn't related to the decision to be made.

In a negotiation about price, the anchor effect means that whatever number is mentioned first becomes the fixed point all further discussions are centred on; perception of value or likely return on investment holds less sway than whatever the first figure bandied about happened to be.

We can also use this heuristic to our benefit by making that first bid and setting the benchmark for future discussion.

Something I want to emphasise here is that I am by no means suggesting that clients—senior, intelligent, and talented people—are making knee-jerk decisions based on biases and cognitive shortcuts. I am saying that knowing that we're all running the same operating system means we can try to remove any likely obstacles between us and that yes. Being easy to buy sometimes means getting out of our own way!

Our brains are processing data in the most energy-efficient (or miserly) way, which is not necessarily the most logical. While we use professional judgment and critical faculties in making decisions, especially in the workplace, we can't ignore the fact that if we want to influence behaviour, to change hearts and minds, we have a clearer shot if we don't have to reset and overcome a potentially negative perception before we even start connecting and building chemistry. If you think about it like a high ball, let's use what we know about how we think and make choices to set ourselves up for success.

For example, the framing effect means that we make different decisions based on how information is presented rather than the information itself. This depends on the offer and the context, but we are more concerned with avoiding possible adverse outcomes than pursuing positive opportunities. Again, it's our brain trying to keep us safe.

A framework I find helpful in thinking about practical actions that influence behaviour change is EAST.

The thinking comes from behavioural economics and psychology. It's also known as "nudge theory," and one reason I like it is that it confirms the rationale for some of the techniques I've developed through decades of experience pitching and working with thousands of clients to polish their public speaking skills.

If you want to influence someone to take any action or change their behaviour or attitudes, make it **E**asy, **A**ttractive, **S**ocial, and **T**imely.

Taking away friction or cognitive strain is an important consideration. It's one of the reasons I'm so obsessed with reducing the amount of information in a presentation and not offering endless choices or variations in the room. We know that asking someone to select from too many options can induce analysis paralysis.

It doesn't make people happier to have more choices; the research tells us that when we finally manage to decide, we're more likely to second-guess ourselves and have a lower level of satisfaction about the purchase. In the context of presenting, making something "easy to buy"—whether that's a product or service or the message you're sharing— is essential.

The idea of attractiveness here isn't about being hot, although it undoubtedly helps. It's about making the decision or behaviour change feel good. How can we make ourselves and our pitch more attractive? Well, refer to Chapters 1 through 24! The CLAIM techniques are all about getting attention, delivering positive experiences, building relationships, demonstrating our likeability, and stepping into a more playful and fun zone wherever we can—and wherever it's appropriate.

Make it social. One of the reasons I focus so much on things like energy, chemistry, reinforcing your ideas with your physical presence, turning a monologue into a two-way conversation, and getting to that place where everything that happens in the room feels live, personal, and bespoke is that these are all ways of creating connection. We want to feel as though we are part of the same team. When my team and I walk into a room, we want to show that we're fun and intelligent and easy to work with—this all happens to be true—and we're establishing a social norm. Our behaviour is inclusive and positive and we're demonstrating social behaviours that act as cues to the audience—that idea of a win-win outcome.

Timing matters. Audiences respond differently to precisely the same information depending on when it is received. It's why we ask for the yes there and then, not after we've left the room.

I find solutions for clients within a specific timeframe, where the impact will happen within X weeks or months. Brains do not love delayed gratification; I always want to look for outcomes that deliver something sooner rather than later. If you're pitching something which is a long-term build or process, think about how you could build in some milestones along the way where we can see positive results in a short while, even if they're only a small part of a bigger picture.

There is an alternative perspective: authority (or

flexing your higher status) plays a significant role in changing behaviour. My take on that is that I want these changes to be intrinsically motivated; I want people to come with me on the journey because they're excited, they feel optimistic, or they feel it's right for them or their business.

I believe it's our job as presenters and idea-makers to try to change behaviour through persuasion, effective communication, and connection. Pull, not push; carrot, not stick.

When you use dominance or coercion—and those are strong words, but that is the reality of what we're talking about—when you scare or threaten someone into doing what you want, when it comes from a place of negativity, scarcity, or feeling that they have no choice, firstly, the moment you stop exerting pressure on them, they're likely to return to their earlier state, and secondly...who wants to be that person?

Influence is a cleaner, more positive, and more enjoyable way of asking people to do what you want them to do.

Here are some techniques for you to use immediately to up the level of influence you'll have when you public speak.

Chapter 17

BODY LANGUAGE AND MOVEMENT

"Tie an Italian's hands behind his back
and he'll be speechless."

—Allan Pease (no, we're not related!)

Body language is the only universal language transcending culture and time.

This chapter is almost a mirror of "Reading the Room." In Chapter 12, we explored how to pay close attention to what our audience is communicating, verbally and nonverbally, and ways we could adapt and respond in the moment.

In this chapter, we'll discuss how we use our bodies to communicate what we're saying (deliberately and unwittingly) and look at how you can use your body, movements, and how you present yourself physically to influence how your audience perceives you, and the role of body language in persuading them to say yes to your ask.

I'll cover key areas, from how you dress to how you move on stage, in a boardroom, and on camera and share techniques to help you put these ideas into action.

1. Clothes Maketh the Meeting
2. Body Talking
3. Throwing Hands

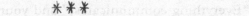

To some extent, we are conditioned not to move freely or naturally in a work setting. While our body language generally helps emphasise the points we are trying to make, it can sometimes have the opposite effect, betraying and undermining what we are trying to communicate.

And, while body language is something that's rarely considered by individuals when interacting with others (the focus is generally on the content of what is being communicated), it is something that humans are incredibly adept at interpreting.

Neuroscientists now understand that speech and gesture are thought to be so profoundly interconnected that gesture plays an essential role in how we think and communicate but is also essential in helping listeners understand and recall the message.[30]

Audiences integrate the information from speech and gesture into a single mental representation, blending these signals into one,[31] making the content more memorable.

I hope by now you're on board with the idea that before you've even uttered a word, people are making judgments about you, often coming to a decision within the first few seconds. Sure, your appearance (height, clothing, etc.) matters, but the subtleties of body language are also constantly being examined and interpreted—as usual, our ever-vigilant brain is on the lookout for any inconsistencies between someone's body language and what they're saying.

Clothes Maketh the Meeting

"Everything communicates," and your outfit says a lot. Wearing a suit in some scenarios can lose the room in an instant. Clothes have their own connotations; a suit might say things like conventional or uncool, depending on the suit, of course.

---

30 Sharice Clough, Melissa C. Duff. "The Role of Gesture in Communication and Cognition: Implications for Understanding and Treating Neurogenic Communication Disorders." *Frontiers in Human Neuroscience.* 2020.

31   D. McNeill, J. Cassell, K.E. McCullough. "Communicative effects of speech-mismatched gestures." *Research on Language and Social Interaction.* 27, 223–237. 1994.

J. Cassell, D. McNeill, and K.E. McCullough. "Speech-gesture mismatches: evidence for one underlying representation of linguistic and nonlinguistic information." *Pragmatics and Cognition.* 7, 1–34. 1999.

The opposite is also true. This is another story I don't emerge from covered in glory, but you learn more from failure than success, so I hope my mistake can save you from crashing and burning.

I recall meeting a senior CEO. My day is often back-to-back with meetings, and on this occasion, I hadn't clocked that I was meeting this CEO until I was already on the road. I arrived at the meeting, and I realised I was wearing an old In-n-Out Burger T-shirt in the lift to the boardroom.

A blank T-shirt communicates casual, maybe even creative. But a slightly tatty, branded burger-joint T-shirt says something far more informal. In this case, I think it might have said, "Zero fucks given."

As I entered the room, I watched the CEO size me up and pause as her eyes alighted on the burger logo. I pressed on regardless. I never asked her, but I believe she felt a level of disrespect like I wasn't taking the meeting (or her) seriously. This was entirely untrue, by the way. The meeting was a bad one and I never made a connection. I'm not saying it was all about my outfit, but it sure as hell didn't help! If I could replay that meeting, I would have had a different shirt on, or failing that, I could have made a reference to my shirt in a self-deprecating way, rather than allowing it to become something of an elephant in the room.

My advice is to wear what makes you feel most in control. But I don't want you to oversimplify this: clothes and fashion are a language, and you can't be in control of the perception of others. Clothes are one of the main ways we can express ourselves to the outside world, although depending on your work culture, you might not have much leeway.

Consider carefully what your outfit communicates and how it positions you. Think about the audience first and foremost.

Consider your subject matter and your context. Are you going to a funeral or a baby shower? Think about what the rest of the room will be wearing. If you're walking into a room full of suits, you should choose your outfit accordingly. This doesn't mean you need to mimic what everyone else is likely to be wearing, but it does mean if you choose to wear a scruffy T-shirt, you need to be conscious of how you'll be perceived.

By all means, wear what you want—wear what makes you feel good, or something that communicates who you are that you think the audience should know—but you will need to do more work to gain trust and influence your audience if you're underdressed or overdressed relative to everyone else. It will cost you some effort, so ask yourself honestly: Do I have the time and skill to do that extra work?

Clothes communicate; our bodies do too. Being intentional about how you move, sit, stand, and so on is something you need to rehearse. Plan how you can emphasise points from your presentation or shift the tone by changing your pose or the pace of movement.

Body Talking

Used with intention, body language is a great way to express yourself. How you move and stand can either tell people you're influential and a master of your content or be a dead giveaway that you're out over your skis.

Use your body language to invite people in—arms open wide, turning your body toward your audience. "Welcome, be part of this, communicate with me. I'm open, I'm honest, I'm transparent. I've got nothing to hide. I've just got value to give and ideas to share."

If you don't plan and practice your movements, your expressions, and your posture alongside your content, there is a good chance you'll be undermining your message without being aware of it.

If you're talking about being open and honest and sharing transparent financial information, yet sitting with your arms folded, chin down, and shoulders hunched, your body language is saying all the opposite things. Most people will listen and watch your body language and take that in as your message, not the words you say, not the things you have on the slide.

Influence is built on trust, and we all make fast judgments. Just as we discussed in the section on voice, using a pitch or tone that's at odds with your words will create a jarring moment, and the audience will feel a loss of trust in you. No trust equals no influence. It's the same with body language.

Think about what kinds of feelings you're trying to elicit in your audience at different points in your presentation. Like everything, you must rehearse. Try doing a run-through where you're doing absurdly exaggerated movements; get feedback from your rehearsal partner about which ones helped give your ideas more heft, and then try a normal version. It's much easier to dial back an over-the-top performance than to boost one that is too understated.

Play with the range. A tiny but strategically timed hand gesture can communicate worlds; sweeping arm movements might illustrate ideas of creativity.

Much like a good film, a good presentation can't be all climax and excitement. It needs quieter and slower-paced moments where you use stillness to draw the audience in and provide contrast with the more impactful, high-energy instances. Identifying where your presentation hits a crescendo, i.e., where you use the most powerful and decisive body language, is paramount.

Whether it's in front of a mirror or camera or, even better, in front of a live audience, practising your body language will only help your performance.

It will help you know whether it's too subtle or flamboyant and whether the timing is correct. Most importantly, it will get you thinking about it, allowing you to analyse your presentation skills as they are happening. And one other thing—if, like virtually everyone starting out, you're not sure whether your body language is too understated or too bombastic, always err on the side of bombastic.

Find a comfortable resting position, then move from that resting position or "home" position outwards to make an expression, use your body to illustrate an idea, and then return to that home. As a default, find a natural, relaxing stance. Everyone's different. I like to have my feet about shoulder-width apart, in a balanced way, and I like to have my hands in front of my body, ready to move as I'm talking because I talk a lot with my hands.

Adapt your movements and gestures for the context: standing on stage, sitting in a boardroom, or on a video call.

Generally, if you're standing at a lectern or on a stage, you can move around at least a little. Just as skilled practitioners know precisely how to use silence, knowing when to move and when to stay still is also critical. In my experience, standing still and delivering from one spot can be a power move. Nervous pacing can communicate nerves whether you feel that way or not.

Some speakers will use the entire stage width, ensuring that all corners of the room get their moment up close with the speaker. They will often start by moving with smaller, slower steps as they build their story, perhaps only glancing up occasionally, as they appear to be concentrating and formulating their argument as they go. The frequency and duration of their eye contact with the audience will increase, and their steps become faster and more deliberate, often complemented with more decisive language delivered at a slightly increased volume. This is an example of what social scientists call a "cluster"—several nonverbal signals layered upon one another to give the audience a richer, more nuanced message.

The audience picks up the changes in body language loud and clear, and the chances of the message hitting its mark are significantly increased.

Obviously, when you're seated, your movement is limited—in many circumstances, big movements might be inappropriate—so leaping to your feet and starting to pace in a board meeting probably won't get you where you want to go.

But even with these limitations, subtle variations in your body language when seated can be used to your advantage.

As you move through your content and want to make a critical point, moving forward in the seat and leaning into the table can help drive the message home with added authority.

You need to gauge this based on your context, but leaning forward and setting elbows on the table can communicate assertiveness and confidence.

Throwing Hands

Tenting or "steepling"[32] your fingers can signal confidence, but an upturned chin plus tented fingers could read as arrogant. Turning the steeple to the side is a move you'll see politicians and lawyers use a lot: it's a mini version of a power pose.

If you can make it work for you, go ahead, but my take is that these contrived and deliberate gestures are hard to blend into a natural flow, and if you can't pull it off, you'll risk coming across like a Bond villain.

Once you've delivered your key point, leaning back in your chair can help communicate openness and willingness to discuss. It can signal that you're waiting for feedback, and you could use this more relaxed posture to show the audience you're open to their questions. Showing that you're at ease is a great way to reinforce confidence, and it also effectively tells the audience you won't do a goddamn thing more until they give you the answers you've asked for.

We've already talked about making eye contact on a video call—of course, the range of expression is even more limited, and the attention of our audience is concentrated on a much smaller area, darting uneasily between eyes and face

---

32   Martha W. Alibali, Dana C. Heath, Heather J. Myers. "Effects of visibility between speaker and listener on gesture production: Some gestures are meant to be seen." *Journal of Memory and Language*, 44, 169–188. 2001. doi.org/10.1006/jmla.2000.2752.

and their image on the screen. Fidgeting or shuffling will seem exaggerated on screen, and these tics can make us feel ill at ease or bored. Aim to keep your facial expressions positive or neutral; we've all seen the eye roll or ill-advised hand gestures from a colleague who temporarily forgot their camera was on.

If you're a hand talker, keep your gestures within the frame. And if you're not a hand talker, try incorporating a few small gestures: research shows people who gesticulate freely are usually seen as warmer, more open, more positive, and more likeable. Try holding your hands loosely with your palms facing up; this is a universally understood signal of openness, trustworthiness, and agreeability.

The important thing to remember about movement is not to do it unnecessarily: every move you make on stage or in a conversation should have meaning. So, if you move toward or away from the audience, make sure it relates to your point.

You don't want body language to be hard work; you want it to be easy and natural because you want to come across authentically.

Bad or forced body language can be highly distracting. Additionally, stilted body language, if it's over-rehearsed, can be distracting as well, where you start doing the same kind of repetitive body language you've learned and rehearsed so much that it now looks robotic and awkward.

It doesn't take much to pull your audience's minds away from your subject matter; instead, they're picking up on that slight whiff of something feeling off, a little inauthentic, and immediately they get a little dose of cortisol. They're instantly thinking about and watching your body movements and body language.

Remember when we discussed the (false) statistic that 90 percent of communication is nonverbal? That research showed that when the audience perceived incongruity between what someone said and what they did, how they moved, or what their body language was indicating, in that instance, the words dropped to around 7 percent of the overall impact and recall.

You want your body language to feel natural and purposeful and help communicate your points.

I like to use my hands to draw my audience's attention visually. If I talk about underlining a point, I may make that gesture of underlining something.

Or if I talk about the concept of a square, I may make that square with my hands.

If I'm talking about high energy, I might lift my hands above my head and maybe step forward. For low energy, maybe I'll crouch and bring the audience down to a lower point. I change my body shape to communicate my points. But that's me—I use large amounts of expressive body language.

I think it's a significant part of self-expression, and I'm comfortable doing that because it's my personality. It may not be yours, and that's cool.

If you think you probably need to use less body language because that's more suited to you, the same rules still apply. Make sure anything you do with your body language and the amount of movement you do onstage or in a room communicates and reinforces your content.

We've already spoken about getting physical, limbering up and moving before you get on stage or into the room. You want to feel like you can be expressive with your body, hands, and face, so stretch before you present. And by the end, it should feel like a physical and mental experience, so you come off stage or leave that room feeling like you've worked out in a positive way.

Find body language that is specific to you, authentically you, but that is also specific to your content and reinforces your points. A phrase buttressed by body language is way more memorable than words alone. Express yourself—and notice how much more engaging you become to the audience with a little more movement.

Chapter 18

TELLING STORIES

"Rule of storytelling: When a character is shoved against a wall, shove them against a wall harder."

—Aaron Sorkin

Stories are how we connect; they're the glue that holds our social groups together. They're how we make sense of the world. Stories are how we share experiences and how we demonstrate our intentions. When we tell a story, we use concrete forms of communication, and our brains have adapted to enjoy that experience.

This chapter examines what happens to the audience when we present ideas using storytelling techniques, and we'll look at some techniques. I'll then take you through three detailed structures for presenting and the use cases for each of these.

1. Structuring Stories
2. A Pitch in Three Acts
3. Layer Cake
4. The Long and the Short of It

I've also added three narrative structures to experiment with at the end of this chapter. Winding Road is my favourite!

One of the most compelling ways to grab and keep attention is to make clear to the audience that you'll tell them a story—and then, of course, you must tell the story. The relationship between storyteller and audience is so well understood that you'll see the audience naturally adopting that position: eyes fixed on the storyteller, single-pointed focus and ready to listen, waiting for you with full attention. That's an influential setup before you've even begun.

It's no coincidence that movies, books, and the urban legends you heard at your granny's knee often share a similar rhythm and structure. An interesting thing occurs in our brains when someone tells us a story. Not only are we instantly alert and ready for the unfolding of the tale, but we're also receptive.

It's that perfect balance of arousal and reassurance: I'm switched on, but I'm also relaxed enough to process information and store memories.

We tend to remember stories more than facts or figures. For most of human history, stories were how knowledge and information were transmitted. When you tell a story, you create a (hopefully) vivid mental image in the listener's mind, making the message more memorable and easier to recall later. Storytelling has existed in every culture, helping us memorably make sense of the world, from what to eat to which peers were available as potential partners. It's thought that storytelling had an evolutionary or adaptive purpose; "it evolved because it offered a benefit in the ancestral environments where it emerged."[33]

There is a tension between the familiar and the excitement of an adventure, so when stories begin with "Once upon a time," we, the audience, get the signal to settle into a state of pleasurable anticipation—or anticipatory pleasure. The storyteller has given us the cue that we are in for an exciting journey. As yet, we do not know what form the journey will take.

We are all natural storytellers. Some of us are more skilled than others, but most are probably a bit out of practice.

We are uniquely fortunate, at this time in human history, to have access to myriad human stories through

---

33 "Storytelling as Adaptive Collective Sensemaking." *Topics in Cognitive Science*— Lucas M. Bietti, Ottilie Tilston, Adrian Bangerter, 28 June 2018.

movies, books, TikTok videos, and TED Talks. So you'll never be short of inspiration or guidance in honing your craft as a storyteller.

There are some key building blocks to storytelling that I want to show you. Suppose you want to go on and read more deeply about this subject. In that case, there are many incredible theorists who take a forensic and analytical approach to the art and science of story—I'd recommend people like Joseph Heller, Christopher Booker, and the wonderful Blake Snyder.

But for the purpose of becoming a great presenter, you just need to understand the fundamentals. And like so many things in this book, we need to learn the rules, and then we can play with them, bend, and even break them. But before we dismantle something, we need to understand how it works.

Structuring Stories

French film director Jean-Luc Godard said films need a beginning, middle, and end, but not necessarily in that order. It might be good for entertainment and win you a few awards, but for the purposes of telling a story in a presentation, other than a few elegant or unexpected twists and turns, the basic structure of your story in a presentation should be erring on the side of simplicity, and I'd probably aim for something linear.

We're not doing this to win the Palme d'Or. We're doing this to win the room.

So, what are the key components of story? The science of storytelling (yes, that's a thing) tells us that there is a universal basic story plot, or pattern, and a million variations of it. You can see this play out in…well, every TV show, film, book, play, or musical you've ever seen.

Firstly, the Anticipation stage; the beginning of a quest, a call to adventure, and the promise of change to come. Then the Dream stage—initial indications of success. Everything seems to be going well, sometimes giving our hero an illusory sense of invincibility.

But wait! Then we move into the Frustration stage, the point of the first confrontation with adversity. Predictably, things begin to go wrong.

It gets worse. Now we move into the Nightmare stage: this is the high point of dramatic tension as we move through the narrative. Disaster has struck, and we begin to fear all hope is lost. But finally, we arrive at Resolution. The hero or heroine eventually triumphs, having learned some lessons along the way. Many movies, novels, and TV shows follow these cycles.

They will sometimes contain only some of these elements, or sometimes the movement through the stages is incomplete or begins again midway through the show, but the cycle is predictable and no less compelling than the fact that we have seen or read this all before.

Think about all the things that happen when you watch a great movie or when you read a great book, the investment you make in the process, the way you empathise with the hero, becoming distressed at the moments of despair and elated when they overcome their challenges. Imagine that happening for your audience when you do your pitch!

If your presentation contained even a tenth of this

emotional intensity, consider how much more deeply your message would land and resonate, and how much easier it could be to get to a yes. Start by printing out, or writing out, your speech. Having it in hard copy will help you see your material as a whole rather than point by point. Then, stand back and start to think about the story behind your facts and figures.

Naturally, you need to find your own real stories to tell, but hopefully these five quick examples show you where to start looking for them.

1. You're pitching to get an investment in your new technology idea in a venture capital boardroom. Instead of talking features and benefits, try taking the audience back to the moment when the idea started. Tell your audience about that moment in detail and help them share that first feeling of inspiration.

2. You're figuring out how to propose to your significant other on holiday. Consider telling them a story about your life before they arrived. Introduce them to that old version of yourself, and don't skip the details.

3. You're asking your boss for a pay rise in her office. Tell a story about how your friends and family feel about you working there. Maybe it's a story filled with positivity... your parents couldn't be prouder. Or maybe they took some time to convince, but they're now the biggest advocates for the job and the business.

4. You're campaigning on a national stage for votes. Try telling your audience about a dream you had (thanks, MLK). A dream about a world where your campaign promises have been delivered. Like in the other

examples, go into the details and make the audience inhabit that new world.

5. You're making a speech at your school reunion. Instead of simply talking about your experiences and the people you knew well, why not tell a big story about why schools exist? You could then pepper that board narrative with specific stories about you and your school along the way.

A Pitch in Three Acts

This is a more nuanced version of the hero's journey. For simplicity and time, if we stick to the classic three-act structure, the narrative arc will move through these three phases: crisis, struggle, and resolution.

How does this work in a pitch? Don't forget, by this stage, you have already set the moral, and now the audience is intrigued and engaged, leaning in with anticipation, waiting for you to bring the story to life.

Firstly—think of this as Act One—you create the setup. In the context of public speaking, now is the time to introduce the situation or setting—also known as the objective and the source of conflict that's getting in the way or preventing your audience from being where they want to go. Here you're establishing the story world or giving the audience the scope of your idea and the framework of your thinking, setting the stage for the main section of the pitch.

But in following this pattern, the next task is to create (or build) curiosity. This could take the form of an information gap, or an inspiration gap.

Any good story needs conflict. It's an essential element;

it builds tension and a sense of what's at stake. These are the forces that drive the plot forward.

The next section is Act Two—or the confrontation. In most dramas, this act is the main body of the story, in which your hero faces challenges and conflicts as they try to achieve their goals. In our context, it's the client's obstacles or what's getting in the way of their commercial objectives.

This act often includes a midpoint, or a turning point, which marks a significant shift in the story's direction.

Act Three: The resolution. This act brings the story to a close, resolving the conflicts and tying up loose ends. This is where you deliver the moral. The resolution could be a satisfying and neat conclusion, or a tantalisingly complex cliffhanger, possibly hinting at further troubles to come—depending on your aims.

Layer Cake

When narrating these stages, it's essential to use a lot of metaphors—a visual or physical way of packing meaning into our words. The brain processes sensory inputs more deeply if they're layered: a description containing sounds and smells and sights has a higher likelihood of recall than just one piece of sensory information alone. Memory (and we'll go deeper into this in Section V) is enriched by associations.

Similes and metaphors create mood, they evoke emotion; they're a shortcut to the audience's existing neural networks, and they help your message sail past the reptilian brain and into the mid and prefrontal cortex.

But...choose your words carefully. Language carries

additional meanings and connections to existing emotions and experiences.

When I say "the smell of a hot car in summer" to you, the chances are it sets off a series of associated thoughts and ideas; perhaps you recall the way the black pleather of the back seat of your dad's Holden, or whatever it might be, stuck to your legs when the thermometer reached thirty. The Magic Tree air freshener dangling from the rear-view mirror gave off a faint scent of synthetic vanilla that always made you feel like you wanted to sneeze.

This is an entirely made-up example, and I used a few well-worn Aussie tropes deliberately—but that's the sort of thing that's taking place in the minds of your audience whenever you're describing something.

Words carry a lot of potency, and this is both an opportunity and a risk: can you be sure you're not using a metaphor that might evoke some unpleasant or negative feelings? Of course, we can't ever know this for sure, but when you're setting out to influence and persuade people to share your point of view, it's handy to be aware of the potential bumps in the road.

In terms of metaphor, just as with humour and everything else I've shared, you'll need to calibrate what you know about the individuals and the organisation based on your reading of the audience.

If you think of metaphors as existing on a spectrum, where one end is sex and violence (very exciting, creating a high level of arousal in the brain and getting the attention of your audience, but also extremely risky), and the other end is "beige tea towels" (extremely safe, and extremely dull), sticking to the middle ground is probably where the smart money bets.

This is nerdy but interesting: in linguistics, one way of looking at how language shapes our understanding of the world is the concept of connotation and denotation.

In simple terms, denotation is a word's literal, or surface, meaning, and connotation refers to the associations and values attached to that word.

Denotation is a fixed meaning, and connotation can vary greatly, depending on your cultural, historical, and social background, lived experience, and so on.

For example, "freedom" has a denotative meaning of being unconstrained, to act without interference. But the connotation of "freedom" can land differently depending on who you are and where you come from. For some audiences, "freedom" might connote an idea of individualism and self-determination, while for others, it might have associations with protest, collective liberation, and social justice.

Like body language, like accents, like everything, there's no single experience shared by all of us. The idea of connotation and denotation is a good way to remind yourself that language isn't neutral. It's helpful to consider the audience and their likely context and experiences whenever possible, but you can't always understand where everyone is coming from.

This is more reason to use the tools we know work, that connect with most people most of the time, and storytelling is a perfect example because it can help to bring everyone onto the same page. By telling a story, you get to define, fill in, and colour many contexts; you set the meaning of the message you're trying to convey. And because stories are built on empathy, that foundation, which is warm and tolerant and seeks connection above all, overcomes a lot of the messiness of our disjointed interpersonal communication.

When your audience hears this message in an emotive format, they are more likely to be convinced by the argument. Emotions, way more than facts, are a powerful motivating force for acting, shifting beliefs, or changing behaviour.

Even if you don't turn your entire presentation into a story or use a tried and tested narrative arc—and I highly recommend you at least try this—you can incorporate story elements in your presentation.

Nine times out of ten, maybe more, you will feel the shift in the audience as they give you their full attention.

In the pattern-making section, we'll discuss how we look for replicable and predictable things. Story structures are universal, and while each one is unique, the overall movement, trajectory, and construction work in deeply understood and expected ways, and that's one of the reasons our brains love them so much.

The Long and Short of It

I recommend you try to hone the narrative of your pitch—moving through the three stages: setup, crisis, and resolution, and then reworking it so that you can pitch the same story in three different lengths.

In the most extended version, you can provide more richness and detail, and pull in all the metaphors and context, seamlessly weaving in the facts about competitors, consumer insight, market forces, whatever it is. That's your conference-room pitch.

Next, try tightening this up. Can you tell that story in less than ten minutes? Determine what's creating impetus, movement, emotion, and tension in the narrative and what parts are window dressing.

You can use this version of your pitch when you run into that sought-after angel investor in a coffee shop, and she agrees to hear you out while she finishes her tea.

And then—and this is undeniably the toughest brief—can you strip it back even further, so you could pitch it during a cab ride across town? This is a great way to understand the essentials versus the fluff. Some parts can't be removed or the whole thing collapses—the conflict section, for example—but you might be surprised at how much you can simplify without losing the power and flow of the pitch.

Using a tried and tested narrative structure gives the presentation a gravity and impetus of its own.

I think you might have guessed where I'm going here: if you can get the meaning, the moral, and your message across in ten minutes, using the techniques of storytelling to keep the audience on the edge of their seats, or at least giving you their attention—do you need the fifty-minute version?

If we want to influence our audience, it's not enough to get our audience's attention; we also need to move them and connect with them on an emotional and empathic level.

By using the storytelling technique, we can tap into that pattern-seeking part of our brains. When we connect through stories, two distinct things happen, both of which get us closer to winning the room.

Firstly, we can communicate our message and our content directly to the neocortex, precisely the part of the brain state we want our audience to be in when we pitch. And secondly, we become more influential and have higher status because the storyteller, by default, is in a position of authority and trust—this is how people have sought explanations for how the world around them works for as long as there have been people.

These techniques will elevate you into that trusted position faster than you can say, "Are you sitting comfortably? Then I'll begin."

If you want your presentation to be engaging, and you want it to be remembered, then you've got to get your head around the importance of storytelling.

Narrative Structures

I've put together three narrative structures for you in this section. They are each specific, designed for different purposes, and have different outcomes attached to them. But what they all have in common is that they use the conventions of storytelling and how the narrative works as a shortcut to create a connection, building trust and influence with audiences.

The key message here is to choose a structure that works for your audience, in that room, on that day.

Narrative Structure One: Drumroll

The Drumroll structure involves building the story to a crescendo. It's the classic structure and starts out slowly and gradually, and over the course of your presentation, your pace speeds up until you get to the point where you will have the reveal.

The key is to take the audience through the content point by point, section by section, increasing the intensity and pace, and signalling a building excitement until you're at fever pitch.

Let's say that for the first twenty minutes, you would have a structure something like the standard first section. What is the context? Why are we here? What are the things in section two we can move toward, tease, and create some anticipation around?

What's changed? What are the complications? What's interesting? What is the potential?

You can already feel the intensity rising as you move through the section. You begin to frame the attention in an escalating pattern: What will go wrong? What is the risk? What is at stake? What could we gain from doing this?

Bring those ideas to life, and get vivid with your descriptions, whatever the situation.

But again, you're taking the audience to a point of tension; they're teetering on the edge. You've gone straight from something reasonably mundane, like the market or competitor context, with swift sideways lurches into what's changed—and then suddenly you're talking about what's at risk, for you, but also for your audience.

You then pause and wait and let that moment sink in. And then, slowly but surely, you walk back down the other side of that hill until you reach your conclusion. In my experience, at this point, the audience is right alongside you every step of the way.

Then you look back to the beginning; come back to the context, what's at stake, why now, and again, you're bookending the front of the deck with the back of your presentation.

When you sense that the energy is building, and their anticipation is palpable, then—and only then—you reveal your idea. Your audience is excited, they've bought in, and they're making emotional connections throughout the story.

The purpose of the Drumroll is all about developing excitement and energy in the room.

There's an undeniable tension and anticipation when you use the Drumroll technique.

Almost any content can be put into a Drumroll structure, but it's perfect when you're still getting to know an audience and cementing that chemistry. Both the Build Back and Drumroll presentation structures are great for new clients or people who are new to you.

Drumroll is a great way to set a tone, feel live and in the moment, and build energy so people are excited about you and your content.

Narrative Structure Two: Build Back

Build Back is the opposite of Drumroll and perfect for those meetings where the audience you're presenting to is a bunch of busy alpha-type personalities. They believe they don't want, or don't have the time, to hear the whole story.

They say things like, "Save the song and dance," or "Just tell me the idea."

In truth, they want to hear your story (they are human,

after all); they just don't want to wait for any reveals or punch lines.

You're probably wondering how that will work. We're all accustomed to the notion that we need to create tension by holding back some information, by building to a moment where we can say, "Ta-da!" with our jazz hands aloft and do a big reveal. No judgment; that's the way most Hollywood movies are constructed.

This is where Build Back can help. At the start of the presentation, you present your idea. No introduction and no preamble. Then you stop talking and sit in silence for a moment. Make eye contact around the room and smile at people. Take a beat and then walk through the background behind your idea. Talk about the research, insights, and breakthroughs along the way.

If your audience is the true alpha type, they'll have questions straight off the top. They will want to talk, which is a great thing. Let them punctuate your story with their comments and questions. We know from Chapter 7 that getting your audience talking is a terrific way to boost your likeability and your likelihood of success in the room.

Then, depending on what happens next—whether the questions keep coming or the audience wants you to present the rest of your message—either it becomes a conversation, or you continue with your presentation and slowly but surely tell them the story behind the idea you presented in the first minute.

I can't recall who said this phrase, but it's perfect for the Build Back narrative structure: "Save the logic until after the magic." When I do a Build Back pitch, I often wonder why

I structure my pitches any other way. The audience gets to feel that their status has been affirmed, and you get to launch your big idea to an audience in a surprising, courageous, and delightful way.

Often you don't even get to do your presentation. Instead, it becomes a big two-way dialogue. You presented your idea at the beginning, and then an organic conversation took over. Questions come up, and you answer them. People ask more questions, and you answer them. That is about as live and in the moment as you can make a presentation.

I bet you're thinking, "How the hell will I make that feel cohesive like a story? How will I get any of my points across?" As with nearly everything in this book, you need to rehearse it.

Narrative Structure Three: Winding Road

Winding Road is about demonstrating empathy and insight.

It's a structure that's ideal for selling complicated or higher-risk ideas. It's also helpful in having difficult but necessary conversations.

Here's how it works: instead of telling a direct, linear story, you take your audience on a winding road from your introduction to your idea. And on that winding road, you have several bends. These bends are where you present the good (but not great) ideas you had during the process of having your great idea—the one you're recommending today.

The structure would look like this:

1. Explain the brief or problem you need to solve.

2.   Start to travel on the winding road and explain the start
     of your process.

3.   Introduce your first idea and explain why it's exciting
     for several compelling reasons. But then explain how
     the first idea hit a series of stumbling blocks and
     demonstrate why this first idea is not the right solution.

4.   Keep travelling down the winding road and describe
     more of your process—maybe some research you did or
     some insights you collected.

5.   Then you introduce the second idea. This felt like the
     right idea. It was great for several reasons, and you
     got all the way to designing it. But then the idea hit a
     different set of stumbling blocks. So, you kept going.

6.   Then you had that "aha!" moment. The stars aligned,
     and you found the perfect idea. And you explain why
     it's a perfect idea—specifically for this problem and for
     this audience.

7.   Explain why this idea solves all of the issues your
     first two ideas illuminated. It's the perfect idea for
     all the usual reasons, but also because it beats those
     other ideas.

The structure offers you built-in objection handling. It is
a powerful way to demonstrate that you've considered all
the obstacles and challenges and done your due diligence in
considering all the angles.

Winding Road is a great structure for getting people to
believe in you and have empathy with you and your content.
It is a brilliant way of breaking down the barriers between the
presentation team and the audience. By showing our hand, so
to speak, we demonstrate a degree of vulnerability.

This is a low-key flex. It's one of those moments where you show how many great ideas you can generate before breakfast without breaking a sweat by laying bare your process. It's textbook Game Theory: you're brimming with so many creative ideas that discarding them out of hand isn't a big deal.

And remember that, for creative people, every idea we have is like a tiny, vulnerable baby that needs our protection. Our instinct is to cherish it—or ruthlessly cull it, sometimes in a rush of self-loathing. Just me?

Above all, this approach requires absolute, cast-iron confidence.

The Winding Road structure means you're not afraid to show the workings in the margin, revealing your process. There's no hiding; it's raw and stripped back, and you're effectively standing naked before the client.

I want to emphasise that, by doing this, we are grabbing a lot of attention and power. The underlying message is to check out the bad ideas I have discarded and get excited about the ones I have chosen to take forward. Let's be brutally candid: you aren't ever including your genuinely unworkable or bad ideas; you're picking your top three concepts, not one great idea and some others you dug out of the bin. But this is all part of the theatricality of pitching.

The benefits of Winding Road are plentiful.

1. It's a great way of demonstrating the depth and breadth of the work you've been doing. You get to show your process and the quality of your thinking. It's not just evidence of industry. You include ideas that were genuine contenders and then explain why you had to discard them and why the final idea is even better.

2. It drives empathy and understanding. Your audience gets to understand the journey you've been on to get to the idea. This is a great way to influence people.

3. It's an engaging way to tell a story. You get to take people on the highs and lows of your process. When done well, the "unthought-known" can occur. This term refers to a phenomenon where your audience doesn't know your idea, and then, once they hear your idea, they feel like they already knew it. This is usually a result of a great Winding Road that gets the audience to imagine the idea before hearing the idea. The audience reacts often, "That's exactly what I was thinking!"

4. It's a great way to get people to realise the pitfalls of other ideas, which in turn bolsters your recommended idea. When you're in a competitive situation, you may want to place the typical ideas of your competitors on the winding road and then explain why they won't work.

Chapter 19

STOP OVERSELLING

"All art is knowing when to stop."

—Toni Morrison

This chapter focuses on what happens when you reach the end of your pitch.

It's a common mistake I've seen repeatedly; people talk themselves out of a yes. I want to explain what's happening at this moment and why and share some techniques to help you avoid falling into this trap.

I'll outline three ways to stop overselling so you can leave that room with your desired outcome.

1. Selling Yourself Out
2. Do You Want Fries with That?
3. Tyres on a Gravel Road

✳ ✳ ✳

When I talk about being influential, it's about exerting a pull more than a push.

You want people to come on a journey with you. While you might be showing them the way and inviting them to take the first step, you need to influence the audience so they can take a leap of faith with you.

Importantly, once they've taken that leap, it's time to stop selling! Simply put, you need to leave them wanting more.

It's tempting to oversell. Maybe the rush of dopamine you get when you're getting all the positive feedback makes you get carried away, or perhaps you get greedy and go for more...or maybe you just can't quite believe it's a yes.... Whatever the reason, you keep pitching even though you've already pitched and won. It's time to say thank you and leave.

Selling Yourself Out

Most people, when they're pitching, have some degree of anxiety or self-doubt. So, even once you've successfully sold your concept and done it well, you want to keep selling to ensure that it has connected with the client. And the irony is that it can have the opposite impact.

Once you've got your audience agreeing with you, and you've got them to say yes, all you can do from that moment onwards is go backward. They are already in, so everything you say from that point on can have no effect or it can start to pick your sails apart. And this can happen in a multitude of ways.

Firstly you can open up your audience for doubt through repetition. They can start to overanalyse as you make the same points over and over. Doing this can take them to a place where they start questioning their first decision.

Do You Want Fries with That?

A second way to oversell is through the introduction of additional new ideas.

I was in a meeting recently where I was pitching alongside a colleague. We were at the end of our presentation, and our idea had landed.

Just as I was about to close my laptop and head for the door, my pitch mate started expanding our idea and bringing in new ones.

The new ideas were great, but we had already gotten a yes! The client was ready to talk about pricing and timelines.

My pitch mate was, and is, an effective communicator, so they introduced these new ideas well. And the client, who mere moments ago had wholly bought our concept, started to say things like, "This is a major program of work with lots of ideas...I wonder where we should start." And, "There are so many aspects to this, I wonder if we have the time and resources to execute properly."

And just like that, this client moved from a **yes** to a **maybe**...and we were scrambling.

We'd done our pitch. We'd rehearsed it. And we executed it. But because we introduced new ideas at the end and new aspects to the lead idea, the client became less confident with their first instinctual decision.

Tyres on a Gravel Road

As I mentioned, when I was a fresh-faced young ad guy in New York, I was lucky enough to work with advertising royalty Phil Dusenberry. He went on to write *The Natural*, starring Robert Redford, and lots of other amazing things. He was an incredible ad man and an incredible human being.

I remember being in rooms with him when he pitched. He would present the idea and then abruptly start walking out of the room.

There was a standing joke about him: "What's the first thing you hear after Phil pitches?"

"His car tyres screeching in the car park."

And that's because Phil knew that once you've done your pitch, presented the idea, and sold it in, all you can do from that point is unravel it and unpick the great work that's just been done.

You need to pitch, and then you need to get the heck out of there.

A concept that we talk about a lot in my office is "Make it easy to buy."

A great pitch makes your ideas easy to buy. It builds belief in your audience and lets everyone know it's achievable. It's affordable. It's powerful and effective.

Do that succinctly and quickly. After that, all you can do is start to plant seeds of doubt.

And those seeds of doubt grow and grow the longer you spend in the room. So, the advice is straightforward: pitch in a succinct way. Tell a story. Get to the end. Give them something to remember and hang on to at the end—then start standing up and getting out of the room.

And I know, for many people, this sounds like an insulting way to behave. But I'm telling you, if you want to preserve what you've created—the buzz, the chemistry, and the golden afterglow of a great pitch—you need to get out of the room.

Simple things like ending the slideshow, closing your notebook, starting to push your chair out, and starting to use language that brings the room to a natural close—are things you need to be actively doing.

And if you're presenting with a group, the rest of your team should be doing it too; you should have already practised it, rehearsed it, and thought about how you will do it.

Ultimately, if everyone in your team acts like this, your audience will follow suit.

And before you know it, you'll be out of the room. In

a taxi, driving away from the meeting with a sold-in idea—rather than hanging around, waiting for seeds of doubt to be planted and blossom. You are waiting for someone to think of reasons why your idea or strategy shouldn't happen.

I get that it seems counterintuitive. People think you want to hang around at the start of a meeting and do small talk; you've built this chemistry, and you want to hang around at the end chatting.

I'm offering up something different here. No small talk at the start. Pitch concisely, to the point, well prepared, and then get out of the room.

Think of it this way: what a gift to the client to have chosen a brilliant idea that will help their business and make them look good to their board, and—as a little bonus, wrapped up with a bow—you're giving them fifteen minutes of their day back.

And we may as well admit it: screeching out of the car park like Phenomenal Phil is a high-status power move; it reminds the client that you're a great asset to their business and that you value and respect their time—as well as your own.

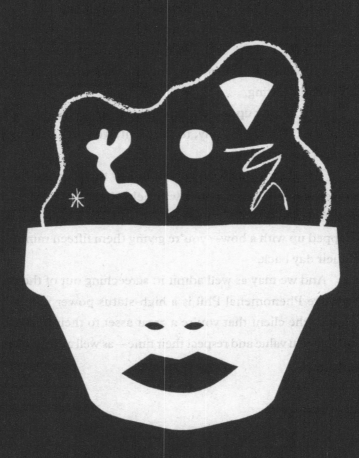

Memorable

SECTION V

Everyone is lazy, distracted, and forgetful...
right up until you show them something
brand new!

One of the goals I set for myself when I pitch is that I want that experience to be preserved in the minds of my audience. The ideas I create should be unforgettable for those on the receiving end. There's no higher honour than being given a permanent space in someone's heart or mind.

Winning the Room is all about being memorable. And I place this element last, as you need to have the rest of the CLAIM model firing before you can achieve it. You've got to have confidence; you've got to demonstrate likeability; you've got to be authentic; and you must structure your presentation in an influential way.

Then, finally, you've got to be memorable: creating and doing things that stick in someone's brain. Whether physical, mental, or visual, you need to do this in a way that ensures you stick out from the crowd.

We live in a world where we are overloaded with stuff: advertising, media, on-demand and catch-up services, stories from everybody all over social media, more emails, more phone calls and texts, six different messaging apps, dating apps, notifications…all that to fit in to your day before you've had a chance to spend face-to-face time with the people who matter at work or at home.

The amount of information we're being bombarded with these days is incredible. Sixty years ago, professionals typically had a secretary to manage their correspondence. Today, we spend over a third of our working days dealing with email, and some estimates say at least 50 percent of this barrage is without purpose. The volume of data created from the beginning of humanity to 2003 was estimated to be 0.5 percent of a zettabyte. And now, the amount of data being produced globally is predicted to reach 180 zettabytes by 2025. Apparently, if each terabyte in a zettabyte were a kilometre, it would be equivalent to 1,300 trips to the moon and back (768,800 kilometres). That analogy is so large to me—I can't even begin to comprehend what a single zettabyte looks like. Let's go with big and overwhelming. It's a lot.

In this context, being memorable is more critical than ever. So, how do you stick out from the crowd in this noisy world? How do you do things that make you memorable? To understand that we need to know what makes something memorable, the basics about how memories are formed, and how our job in a pitch is to create ways for the message to move from short- to long-term memory.

I want to explain how memory works from a brain science point of view to give you the context to understand why and how the techniques work.

You may have heard of the so-called lizard brain theory,[34] which says that the human brain is composed of three parts: the reptile brain, which governs basic survival; the limbic, which controls emotions and memories; and the neocortex, which is our higher-order thinking. Each part of the brain supposedly evolved sequentially, affecting behaviour and decision-making differently. It's now understood to be wildly oversimplified. However, the fact we still frame our thinking and cognitive processes in this way shows you that using highly memorable elements can make an idea almost indelible.

---

34 "Your Brain Is Not an Onion with a Tiny Reptile Inside." Joseph Cesario. orcid. org/0000-0002-1892-4485 cesario@msu.edu, David J. Johnson, and Heather L. Eisthen.

Understanding how memory works means we can intentionally craft content that's easier for our audiences to recall. When we recall something, what takes place on a neurological level is a reactivation of the interlinking, connected neural circuits containing pieces of the information which make up that memory. Memory is almost like experiencing the thing all over again.

First, the core principle of memorability is association. So, the likelihood of an idea remaining in people's minds long after you have left the room has a lot to do with how vividly and effectively you created associations with that idea.

Looking at neuroscience to explain the factors that create a memorable idea from association techniques, we could use the analogy of a tapestry. The richness and tactile nature of the fabric is because it's made up of multiple intersecting threads, all differently textured and coloured. Extending this to language, if you think of the most enduring idioms and phrases—and this holds true in any language— they tend to be phrases that work on several sensory levels.

We talk about painting a picture with words; with that simple example, you can see the appeal to all the sensory-processing centres of the brain. These simple words can evoke so much. You can imagine the texture of the canvas, see the brushstrokes that form the painting, and the colour and depth of the pigment; you can almost smell the paint.

A great tool to assist in improving memorability, and a brilliant way of thinking about the process of memory formation, is the Palace of Memory. Also called "the method of loci"—placing memories in space and time—this technique is a metaphor for a system of memory that allows easier storage and faster retrieval of information by "locating" it and organising it around a virtual or imaginary mental map, usually of a real place.

This kind of memory system has been used for thousands of years. This practice was used by indigenous peoples all over the world, and it's one of the ways Australia's First Nations people could travel from place to place across vast distances, finding food and shelter and meeting other groups. It's also the reason that when you walk into a different room, you can find you've forgotten what you came to do— until you walk back into the original space. Memory and location have a strong relationship.

In the Palace of Memory, each room can hold a different category or type of information. Imagine yourself walking through (imaginary) rooms and placing objects, symbolic or otherwise, in specific places. Then you can easily recall the information by visualising yourself walking through rooms, or the bush, and retrieving what you need.

Second, how our brain shows us things in our memory often differs from the original object. Memory is the constellation of connected, linked neurons representing sights, sounds, language, and all the other sensory inputs.

In 2016, Derren Brown famously tricked a couple of top advertising creatives in London with subliminal persuasion. Derren invited the creatives to his office and gave them a creative assignment. What they didn't know was that Derren had littered their commute with subliminal images that would later inform or inspire their creativity. After an hour of creative work time, the result was that the ideas the creatives came up with were almost identical to the ones that Derren had drawn out prior to their arrival, thus leaving them thinking they were embarrassingly unoriginal. Goes to show when it comes to writing ads, you create what you recall!

And third, if you only remember one thing, remember this: Memory formation requires attention. We remember only what we notice. I'll leave this one right here because much of the content you've already read focuses on this principle.

There are three distinct ways to be memorable: we must create a sense of novelty through shock or surprise, create an emotional connection, or repeat the information.

If we want to help people remember us or our ideas, information needs to be presented in a way that is novel to get our attention—but it needs to arrive when our brains are both receptive and relaxed. A jump scare gets your attention, but the stress would inhibit memory formation. The hippocampus is the part of the brain where memories are formed. The bad news is that stress and anxiety inhibit the development of new neurons in the hippocampus—stress that continues for a prolonged period can shrink this area.

When we're public speaking, we need to find this delicate balance between making our audience feel a lack of stress, ensuring they're receptive to our message, and being edgy and engaging enough to get them to pay attention from start to finish. We've created the foundation for others to feel positive about our content through developing our skills. Our job is to deliver the compelling content they'll discuss after we've left the building, tyres screeching.

When the brain experiences stress, short- and medium-term memories are less likely to be created. Stress negatively impacts memory—both your ability to retrieve information and your ability to make memories.

The reason this section comes last is that getting people to remember your ideas hinges on them liking you, trusting you, and believing in you.

Hearing a great idea from someone we don't like feels unpleasant. Cognitive dissonance, or internal conflict in the realm of ideas, causes us a level of physiological stress similar to experiencing a physical threat.

Memory isn't only an individual experience. For example, many of us can remember a complex network of associated sensory and emotional pieces of information that we associate with, say, the death of a celebrity. Many of us remember vividly where we were, who we were with, and what we were wearing on the day the planes flew into the World Trade Center, and often if you ask someone to recall an event of global significance, they will recall aspects that are second-hand or collective impressions mingled with their first-hand recollections.

Understanding that memorability is derived from connections across different parts of our brain, it's important to think about weaving rich, sensory information around the description or idea you are trying to convey.

I will repeat this to prove a point: To be memorable means content needs to be emotional, surprising, or often repeated.

Chapter 20

THE POWER OF PERP

"The eight laws of learning are explanation, demonstration, imitation, repetition, repetition, repetition, repetition, repetition."

—John Wooden

PERP is a circular model that should be applied to any point you want your audience to recall. It stands for:

Make the **P**oint.

Explain the point.

Repeat the **P**oint.

It is a simple way to drive repetition—as we've discussed, a key component of memorability—without coming across as boring. I developed this over time, and ever since I've been using it, I have seen a solid upturn in how easily people can recall my content in meetings and presentations.

I'll talk more about ways to simplify your content to drive optimum recall in the remainder of this section, but the beauty of this technique is how straightforward and effective it is.

If you don't PERP it, they will forget it.

Looking back at the chapters you've read so far, you might notice that I've used this method regularly. Yes, it works for the written word too! And I hope the fact that you can remember the material is a strong indication that this is a brilliant way to make your points stick in the mind of your audience.

We always have things we want to land when we speak in public. We need our audience to understand these points and, most importantly, to remember them. If you're a mother speaking to a group of tweens about crossing the road safely, maybe you want them to remember to stop at the curb, look both ways and finally cross the road directly—no dawdling!

If you're a chef speaking to your kitchen staff about meal prep, maybe you want them to remember always to preheat the plate, add your signature garnish, and finally, double-check the details of the order before it makes its way across the pass and toward the guest's table.

If you're a CEO speaking with your leadership team during a crisis, maybe you want them to think about reducing risk across the business, doubling down on your corporate social responsibility strategy, and finally showing real empathy for your customers at this difficult time.

The examples are endless; on every occasion, the onus is 100 percent on the presenter to do the work and help the audience know exactly what they're meant to be remembering.

It's so easy for an audience to get lost in your presentation. Even the most charismatic public speakers can leave the audience inspired but still confused.

Usually, the group of people in your audience is there for the right reason. They want to hear from you and believe they're in the right room. You've also hopefully designed your content with your audience in mind. If the match between your message and your audience is working for the most part, why is it so hard to get them to recall your message after you've left the room?

It's not because they're disinterested, and it's not because you're a terrible public speaker. It often boils down to information overload. Winning the Room is all about grabbing attention and then delivering your message in a way that cuts through, holds attention, and hangs around in the audience's memory.

PERP is a simple technique that will increase the

memorability of your points.

Let's talk about your content before we get into the technique itself. Great content starts with sacrifice. PERP is an excellent technique to force you to be disciplined with your content. To cut through the noise in the room, you often have to cut out the noise of your content.

Figuring out what your three to five significant points are is crucial. This distilling process takes a lot of work to do. We often think we have lots of vital points to make. The truth is that your audience will only be able to retain up to five points. For those who truly believe they have more than five significant points to get across, I suggest creating a leave-behind document or a simple summary email that captures all of these points. Then, in your public speaking moment, you can focus on the top three to five and land these in the room.

You could say many things in your presentation but only focus on what will move the needle.

Public speaking is one of those less-is-more situations. My key piece of feedback to nearly every public speaker I work with is to say less. I know removing points is tricky; you're passionate about every point. Moreover, we're obsessed with completeness. The idea of leaving something out often feels like a nightmare for people but give yourself a gentle pep talk: you can always send over additional material, and you can always offer a folder of takeaways, but how you communicate in that unique and never-to-be-repeated live moment is vital.

Here's an example of the power of PERP in practice.

P stands for Point. Make the Point. This is where you clearly state the point. For example: "Swim between the flags."

E stands for **Explain**. Explain the Point. This is where you elaborate on your point and bring it to life for your audience. For example: "When you're at the beach today, please only swim in the area between the flags. These are the only areas that have the full attention of the lifeguards. The ocean can be dangerous, and the lifeguards can only keep you and your family safe if you swim in this specific beach area."

RP stands for **R**epeat the **P**oint. This is where you clearly state the point again.

"It's essential that you always swim between the flags."

A healthy pause between sections will make your point memorable and easy to digest.

That's what one PERP looks like. Now, think back to your full collection of points in your presentation. You've got three to five major points; each one should now have the PERP model in action.

Zooming even further out, let's consider your entire presentation. It's not just your points that you want your audience to remember; it's also the theme behind your entire presentation. I guess you could call it the why behind your presentation.

I recommend a larger PERP around the entire presentation. What I mean by this is that your introduction is the P, where you state what the whole presentation is about, a simple and succinct headline of your presentation.

Staying with the lifeguard example, it could look like this: "I'm here to talk to you about a subject that means a lot to me: staying safe on the beach this summer."

Then E is where you detail what your presentation is about, basically telling your audience what you're about to tell them. I like to mention each of the major points in this explanation.

For example—I will cover three key points.

1. What to take to the beach,
2. Where to swim along the beach, and
3. Who to contact if something goes wrong.

These are my key points today, and I'd like you to look out for them as I move through my presentation.

Then, RP is where you repeat your presentation's theme or overarching point. For example, "By the end of my presentation, you will all understand how to keep yourselves and your loved ones safe at the beach this summer."

Can you feel the power of PERP?

PERP is a simple but incredibly effective technique to boost memorability by repeating what we're going to do, repeating the key points, and then restating what we did.

Chapter 21

SIGNPOSTING

"I have always believed that writing advertisements is the second most profitable form of writing. The first, of course, is ransom notes."

—Phil Dusenberry

Signposting has a simple premise: When you present, your audience needs to know what to remember. It involves breaking down your presentation and the things that come out of your mouth in a way that telegraphs exactly what and when you want them to write down and remember.

I'll explain why this increases recall and give examples of the technique in practice.

We've all heard the saying or the rule: Tell them what you're going to do, do it, and tell them again. Well, that's a positive one.

You begin with your well-honed introduction, and as you explain that you're here to talk about whatever the subject of your proposal might be, as you get to the first key point before you go on, you make a recommendation—you can frame this almost as a directive, which is:

"Write down what I'm about to tell you. It's important. It's worth remembering."

"Get out a notebook and write it down. I'm about to present something important, and it's worth remembering."

Then tell them that point.

You've made the point; you point a signpost back at it. And you say, "Great. I just presented this point; I'd recommend you write it down; it's important to remember." The audience then writes it. Then, after you've made the point, you stick up another signpost, pointing back to the point, and say, "Right, that was point two. This is fun, right?

Have you written down a bunch of information?"

Then you pause. "Okay, so now, I'm going to tell you point three, something specific about that point, why it's worth remembering."

Make that point. Then again, pick up a sign pointing back at that point, and you tell them why you told them what you told them and why it's essential.

And on you go.

In any great presentation, there are three to five major points. Any more than that, you should write it down and send it in an email. Any less, and you're doing yourself a disservice in making the most of that live opportunity. A presentation with this approach is structured. It's full of reminders. It's full of directions. People know exactly what you want them to remember.

One reason this works so well is that people write down only the parts you want them to pay attention to. The other reason is that you're creating extra processing focus on those points, and by asking the audience to write them down, they're getting a multi-layered sensory experience of that content. The sound of your voice, the feel of the pen in their hand, the whisper of the pen across paper, the sight of the words in their almost indecipherable handwriting, and the movement of arm, hand, and fingers in writing down those points all combine to create that constellation of linked neurons. When they come to reread those notes, a different part of the brain is activated than when they skim printed material, which also reinforces memory formation and keeps our brains in that cognitive processing mode.[35]

Now we want to think about what to put on the slide, where your key three to five slides relate to the signpost.

I would offer an introductory thought-provoking slide up front, then three to five slides that are signposts for each point you can make; a slide that reminds the audience that nobody asks for permission for membership or whatever you're trying to get to as that outcome.

And then, finally your last slide—that's a perfect seven to ten slides. All this could be delivered mainly with a few words on a slide; everything else comes out of your mouth.

Everything else is conveyed through your body language. The way you say things, the tone you create in the room. Other than the intro and conclusion, your slides are signposts for what you want people to remember. Otherwise, you're asking the audience to make a lot of notes, and no one's got the attention span.

I'm sorry to break it to you. No one's that interested in your presentation. Yes, they are in the room for a reason, but you need to make it easy to remember, recall, and pass on to someone else.

In practice, I would do this process when you're about to write your speech after you've got your ideas together but while you're still wondering exactly what your timing should be like. At this point, I would then look through my speech and identify the major points. I look for the things I want to accentuate and get my audience to think about and

35   Pam A. Mueller, Daniel M. Oppenheimer. "The Pen Is Mightier Than the Keyboard: Advantages of Longhand Over Laptop Note Taking." *Psychological Science*, 25(6), 1159–1168. 2014. doi.org/10.1177/0956797614524581.

remember, then build it and pause.

And what that means is I'll often write out my speech, and then before and after those points, I will put, "…".

That indicates to me, as I'm giving my speech and saying these words out loud, that I can do a significant pause before and after those moments.

Now, when you pause, a few things happen. Firstly, you, as a speaker, get a moment to take in the audience, have a look around, and enjoy the present moment.

That's a real benefit for you and the way you're going to perform, but also for the audience. They get a moment to think about what you're saying, then get ready for a point. And after a while, with this pause, point, pause rhythm that you get into, your audience will look out for those pause moments. And will then be ready for your point. And will be ready to concentrate on what you say directly after a pause. It also lets the audience know that you're in control. You're not rushing; you've got time to pause. You've got the confidence to pause during your speech, rather than madly running to the end of your presentation.

You're taking the time to pause; let the point sink in. And the more I present and the more I watch team members present and clients present, the more I realise that we just don't pause enough. Even the biggest pausers in the world do not pause enough. If we are in the attention game, which I must tell you we are, especially with the world as it is, so jumbled up with information and noise, we all need to be trying to grab and hold attention more often. Pausing is a big way to do that.

And I don't think you can do it enough.

That's also the moment when we use eye contact, intentional body language, or maybe where you use a bold slide, or some props, right in those pause moments.

The rule, or the tip, is simple: if you want someone to remember something you're about to say, make sure you build up to that moment.

Then you pause, make the point, tell the audience what to capture, signpost back to it—and then pause again afterwards.

And in both of those pauses, before and after your major point, you need to make sure you look at your audience, use all the other things we've discussed in this book during that pause moment, and use your presence to reinforce the point.

Chapter 22

PEOPLE ARE PATTERN MAKERS

"History doesn't repeat itself,
but it often rhymes."

—Mark Twain (allegedly)

This chapter is about the need to deliver your content in a way that capitalises on the pattern-making drive that governs how our brains make sense of the world.

I'll talk you through some of the brain science and offer you some techniques to practice.

If you can make sure that you deliver your presentation using these techniques, you'll increase the chances that your audience will remember the content. Because we *like* making patterns, you'll be giving them content in a way that they find enjoyable.

The techniques I'll cover relate to how your presentation should feel:

1. Novel
2. Narrative-based
3. Visual
4. High-Contrast
5. Short

Our brains are wonderful, miraculous things, capable of empathy and understanding, nuance and complex abstract thought. And they're also built for efficiency: trying to make sense of the world with the least possible effort. It follows that we would rely on a lot of heuristics or mental shortcuts, especially in this age of overstimulation. And knowing this, we can adapt the way we present information to work with the pattern-making makeup of human beings.

You may have heard of the famous experiment that a person looking at a black dot on a blank white wall will notice it, but when they move their gaze slightly away from the black dot, the brain will helpfully "clean up" the wall so that only white is seen.

In a slightly controversial experiment called "the Ganzfeld Effect," a German psychologist named Wolfgang Metzger found that if you deprive the brain of outside stimuli by placing the participant in a total-sensory-deprivation environment, the brain begins to create auditory and visual hallucinations in as little as seven minutes. Our brains need—they love—to be entertained; if nothing is forthcoming from the outside world, we'll invent it. But we are also strongly driven to make sense of the world, to find meaning and predictability where there may be none.

There's something here for the public speaker: serve your content to the audience in ways that the brain will find delightful and compelling, or you might lose them to a world of their own imagining.

There is no better illustration of our obsessive drive to make patterns than the phenomenon of pareidolia, the tendency to see something meaningful in a random or ambiguous visual pattern—usually faces.

Pareidolia is a strange neurological projection most of us experience from time to time, where our brains try to make sense of the world, drawing on past experiences to make predictions to tidy up what we see. The fact we try to find faces in burnt toast, dustbin lids, clouds—or whatever else—is almost charming; you could see it as evidence of our deep desire to connect with one another.

It's an example of our pattern-making impulse. Superior pattern processing (SPP) enables myriad brain functions, including intelligence, language, imagination, invention, magical thinking, and our belief in imaginary entities such as ghosts. Analysing the available data carefully to see if a pattern exists or if we're projecting meaning and predictability onto a random set of disparate stimuli is not how our brains work.

Again, this has its origins in our ancestors' strategies for survival. Scanning a hostile environment and detecting any sign of threat required the brain to be exceptionally good at grouping and categorising stimuli quickly. Is movement in the shadows a predator, or just the wind? The early *Homo sapiens* who hung around to find out for sure were probably not the ones who survived. Thinking about it, the history of our species probably means that our ancestors were the most paranoid members of the tribe, who were the best at running away. I don't know if that's why we're such an anxious bunch these days, but there might be something in it.

Our attention is limited, and our senses deceive us. The eye has a *literal* blind spot, but our brains cheerfully make up a version of what could plausibly fill in that blank space in the retina and tell us that's what we're seeing. We talked earlier about mentalising, or the theory of mind, as applied to ourselves and others: this is another example of our pattern-making compulsion. We can create complex and intricate stories about other people and situations we encounter on almost no data, purely driven by a predictive mental model that tells us things we've seen in the past are likely identical to what's happening now.

Daniel Kahneman explains that the brain has two types of thinking or decision-making processes, which he calls fast and slow, or systems one and two.

System one operates quickly and automatically; it

takes little or no effort, and we have no sense of voluntary control over this process—this system leaps to conclusions and biases and is in charge 98 percent of the time. System two is the process of slow, effortful mental activities that we must deliberately carry out, including complex computations. This is how we make decisions a hefty 2 percent of the time.

How can we use this information to help us engage audiences?

The principles are as follows:

You must make your presentation novel, narrative, visual, high-contrast, and short.

- **Novel:** Give the audience something they haven't encountered before. I'd argue that this should be novel in a positive way; you'd need to have some compelling reasons to deliver something new and unpleasant (remembering that stress impedes memory, and we're certainly not going to be seen as more likeable and trustworthy if we give our audiences a horrible experience).

- **Narrative-based:** Use your storytelling skills to build a presentation that includes a narrative arc; this is code that unlocks our most receptive state of mind.

- **Visual:** While not everyone processes information in the same way, remembering that change is what we pay attention to, creating a bold and eye-catching presentation is a fast and easy way to capture attention.

- **High-Contrast:** Change is what we pay attention to. Whether it's rushing from one section to the next, shifting tone, using movement, or sudden changes in the pitch of your voice, making sure your presentation has moments of dramatic contrast is a great way to keep your audience focused and engaged.

- **Short:** This is relatively self-explanatory. If the meeting is booked for an hour, plan your presentation to run for twenty minutes. Our brains are overloaded, and sustaining attention for lengthy periods of time first creates cognitive load and then cognitive drift.

While it's true that we're sense-seeking and pattern-making as a species by default, it's also important to remember that a growing body of research into neuroplasticity tells us that we are capable of extraordinary levels of growth, adaptability, and change.

There is a theory that one of the best ways to maintain healthy cognitive function is to take on new information continually and try to develop new skills.

Another reason to practice everything you've learned in this book!

Chapter 23

SHIFT THE TONE IN THE ROOM

"True originality can't begin until you know what you're breaking away from."

—Blake Snyder

Every moment (and meeting) you walk into has an existing tone.

Call it a vibe check. There is a distinct energy and a defined rhythm.

It's sometimes hard to put your finger on it, but the tone is everything. When you get the tone right, you will connect, engage, and be memorable. And if you get the tone wrong, as good as your ideas may be, as good as you may be, it can fall flat just purely because you got the tone wrong and, significantly, you didn't shift the tone.

This chapter goes into the need to disrupt the dominant energy in a room, whatever that room may be, as soon as you walk in, and why it's important. I'll teach you how to do that with these techniques:

1. Fifteen Seconds
2. Silence Has So Much to Say
3. Move the Meeting
4. Get Emotional

Let's try an experiment: I want you to take a notebook and a pen: sit quietly for a moment. And then I want you to set a timer, and for one minute, write down every thought that crosses your mind; anything at all that arises, no matter how trivial, any fleeting idea, sensation, memory, whatever it is.

And then I want you to go through and mark every idea or thought that takes place in the past. Then go through one more time and mark in a different colour, or maybe underline, every single thought about the future; something that you are considering, a plan, a dream, something that hasn't happened yet.

Then I want you to have another look, and this time underline each thought that is about the present moment: a sensation you felt, a sound you heard at that second outside in the street, a physical feeling of discomfort that you were observing, anything that was happening at that moment.

Then consider the balance between past, future, and present thoughts.

If that's what our brains are doing—even in a quiet moment of reflection—consider how noisy and busy the brains of all the people walking into the room to hear your pitch are likely to be.

It's a workday; they're preoccupied, thinking back to what happened in the meeting this morning or the petty argument they had with their partner before they left the house; maybe they're trying to remember who's taking the kids to sports this evening.

What are they going to have for dinner? Did they remember the milk? What did the email from Susan in accounts mean? What do they think about you? What is your reputation? What do they think about the subject matter?

This thought experiment is helpful as a way of reminding us we have a lot of work to do in competing with all that mental chatter, and that's the role of shifting the tone: to disrupt the status quo and grab attention by creating change.

Beyond being just a move to generate attention to the present moment, you also need to be conscious that whenever you get onto a stage, walk into a room, or sit around a cafe with a group of people; a tone already exists, usually informed by the people in the room, their relationships, their interactions, and the room itself. All of these things combine to create a tone.

There may be times when the existing tone will not give your presentation the best chance of success. An example of tone could be that it's an unreceptive room, or maybe it's quite a lazy, sitting-back-on-its-laurels kind of room. Or perhaps it's an argumentative, discontented "We want something to break and change" mood. And that means that, whatever you say to us, we're going to try to break and change it. Or maybe it's a cheerful room, where people are thirsty for new ideas and can't wait to build upon what you've got to say. Anyway, the point is, whether you realise it or not, that room, whatever room you're about to walk into, has a tone.

Most people accept the tone in the room that is there when they get there, and then they just have to work with what they've got, whether that tone will support the content they're presenting or create a level of cognitive dissonance. As we've discussed previously, a brilliant idea presented by someone we don't like, however right or effective that idea is, will generally be rejected.

And this translates to tone as well. If someone is in an unreceptive state of mind or having a bad day, they will not clear the mental space required to give your pitch their open-minded attention. If you don't shift the tone, you'll be working with the hangover of whatever their previous interactions were.

In a book like this, I would be generalising to tell you the right tone, because I humbly believe the tone is bespoke to every subject matter. It would be irresponsible to talk about what a great tone might be.

Now, something often misunderstood with this tip or technique is that people think there's an ideal tone to which you need to shift it. Some perfect state in which everyone obediently sits receptively waiting for your pearls of wisdom? Have you met a human?

My advice is simple—and it might sound counterintuitive, but there is no ideal tone to shift it to. You just have to shift it. You could shift it to a more reflective tone if it's a cheerful room. Or if it's a reflective and pensive audience, you could shift it toward a positive higher energy tone. It doesn't matter what tone you shift it to, as long as you shift it.

Obviously you want that tone to play to your advantage in the context of the subject matter you're going to be talking about, but the point is not to get to a perfect tone because there is no such thing. Instead, you just need to shift the tone. Disrupt and reset the energy.

Now, why is that important? Well, we all go through our lives having these meetings, these coffee chats, sitting in boardrooms, listening to representatives, going to a conference, listening to someone on a stage do a keynote—and often, we bob along, relatively unengaged. We arrive with our tone, and we leave with our tone, unaffected and unmoved, and we're never genuinely impacted by the presenter or the public speaker.

The quickest way to break through that is to engage with people, and get them to realise this is something different; the way you signal that this is something and someone that you need to pay attention to is to shift that tone. There are several ways you can shift tone, and I'll list a few of my favourites.

Changing the tone is a deliberate step you need to take,

and below I've outlined a few of my favourite strategies you can use to make an impact.

Fifteen Seconds

It's your job as a presenter to shift the tone in the first couple of minutes. I want to give you a stretch goal: can you change it in fifteen seconds?

That first fifteen seconds is when your audience is most mentally active. They are assessing you and judging your every move. Shifting the tone early communicates that you are in control, you are confident, and most importantly, you are worth remembering!

Silence Has So Much to Say

There are nonverbal ways to shift tone: for example, you can start the meeting with silence.

You enter the room, and you don't say anything. You allow the silence to linger. Then, you look around the room, smile at people, and make lavish amounts of eye contact. In doing this, you create a nonverbal moment that lets people know this is going to be a more intimate, personality-driven meeting and engaging in a way that everyone needs to be personally involved and invested in.

That's probably different from what people were expecting when they hit "accept" on your meeting invite or when they agreed to come and have coffee with you. They probably didn't know it was going to be so challenging. Engaging, yes—the classic passenger experience of sitting and tuning out; that scenario, they were anticipating.

Get Emotional

A verbal way is to start with a story that takes people somewhere emotionally. For example, if you're talking about needing a pay rise, maybe you would start with a story all about the importance of money, or perhaps the unimportance of money, but the reason it matters in this situation. Maybe you tell a story about your upbringing or a job you've had in the past and its impact on your life.

You tell that story to shift the tone and disarm people and let the audience know this is different. This is not a typical chat about a salary review. This is something different, with a different tone. And most importantly, it demonstrates to your audience that you are in control of the meeting, and you have the skills and the awareness to shift that tone. Because that's not a "normal" or conventional way to present.

People accept this situation as a foregone conclusion, the default state of play, immovable and set in stone, and then they do their best to work with that tone.

What I'm suggesting here is you do the opposite. You figure out upfront what tone you want to create in the room, and you also do some research: try and understand what the tone might be in the room. You know, based on your audience, how they feel about the subject matter and how they feel about you.

Purposely design an introduction to reset their expectations and shift tone in the first two or three minutes. You intentionally create a setup that does a circuit-breaker on that existing tone and makes the tone what you want it to be.

Move the Meeting

Another way to shift tone is to move the meeting into a location that reflects and brings to life your content if your subject matter is all about the ocean...pitch at the beach!

If you're presenting an idea about—let's say—the need for middle school students to spend more time in nature, is a stuffy boardroom the setting that will best reinforce your points? Or, if you're pitching a concept for improved accessibility in shopping centres, could you move that meeting to an interesting place that demonstrates your points?

A story I love—advertising pitch theatre at its finest—is the tale of an agency pitching for a rail network account in the UK, famously the home of the worst train services in the developed world. The client was invited to the agency's offices for the presentation and arrived to find the waiting room empty, not enough chairs, litter everywhere, and no sign of the pitch team.

The client became more and more annoyed, and at the exact point when they were about to walk out, the pitch team entered the room and explained that this is the type of experience that rail customers put up with every day, and the remainder of their pitch contained their ideas to improve matters. As you can imagine, that tone shifted significantly, and the agency won the retainer.

If you remember to shift the tone—and keep shifting it—then you stay in control of the room, keep the attention, and create a more memorable moment for your audience.

Chapter 24

SAY MORE WITH LESS

"Before you leave the house,
look in the mirror and take one thing off."

—Coco Chanel

Saying more with less is all part of being memorable.

This chapter is all about brevity. Why is brevity important? We all overexplain and over-present our material; in any context, around a chat, coffee, relationship, or presentation, we say way too much.

Reducing the content creates space for our audiences to connect with the idea. Using the following techniques, I want to show you that you don't need to throw in the kitchen sink to be effective. Work with the capacity of the brain and deliver a presentation that is truly unforgettable and easy to buy.

And if we were critical, and if we rehearsed enough, we would realise we could cut half of our presentation and still convey the same ideas; the difference is that they would hit with a lot more impact because they wouldn't be clouded and confused by the bulk of information that is usually in people's presentations.

1. Pathway to Pitch
2. Strategy Is Sacrifice
3. Eight Minutes

✳ ✳ ✳

As the famous saying goes, "I didn't have time to write you a short letter, so I wrote you a long one."

Brevity takes time; writing something pithy and short takes more effort than writing the long-winded, unedited, sloppy version. And the exact same thing goes for public speaking: it takes a lot more time to create a tight, punchy presentation, all killer, no filler, versus how long it takes to create a flabby presentation, with lots of extra bits that meander around, as opposed to striking a chord and making a solid, distinctive point or points.

This technique is all about being discerning with the choices you make. Once you've chosen what stays, you must make the content you select work hard. Interrogate your content. Look at it in the rehearsal phase, or even before that, and have a clear-eyed, almost ruthless analysis of what might be extraneous. Figure out if you could make any of these points with fewer words. Could you combine two points and remove one?

Could you say it with a visual or some other prop, rather than filling it up with words? And in my experience, often the answer is yes. The ideal presentation is under ten minutes.

There's lots of science around how long audiences can maintain attention, and how long you can hold their focus as a speaker. Neuroscientists suggest it's around ten minutes. Most pitches tend to cover a subject that needs more time, some explaining, and some rigour.

Most of us are probably pitching at an hour. And that is way too long. It's too many ideas. It's not easy to buy. It's not easy to take out of the room for the audience. How do you expect them to walk away and explain it to others when they have to recall fifty-five minutes and seventy slides? We need to be punchier, and pithier, and we need to be more succinct.

The convention of an hour-long presentation is ripe for reinvention. Perhaps the sections covering complexity and outlining the approach could be handled via a pre-read, and then the pitch team swoops in and drops the solution within ten minutes. It's a golden rule I've developed in my own work. I only ever design twenty-minute pitches. The rest of the time is for conversation.

Here are some approaches to how to say more with less.

Pathway to Pitch

In the rehearsal phase (see Chapter 14 for more detail) when you're structuring your presentation, write out your major points, one headline per page, and then print them out on A4 paper.

Then take those A4 pages, and lay them out on the ground or along a large table like a path. That path is your current presentation flow.

Then interrogate every page. Firstly from a helicopter view—reading the headlines in order. Get a feel for how that flows. Then go deeper and discuss each idea on each page in detail. Determine if you can reorder some, remove some, combine some points with other points—or at the least, say it with fewer words. Or maybe you could make a point with a visual, gesture, or piece of music—anything other than more words.

This takes discipline and critical thinking because throwing the kitchen sink into every presentation is a lot easier.

Resist comments or feeling like, "Will they understand how much work we've done if they can't see our three hundred slides? Is this enough (am I enough)?"

It's scientifically proven that our brains can only maintain attention for a few minutes. And the indications are that this attention span is getting even shorter; the proliferation of content and digital noise is driving shorter attention spans and an increasing inability to stay focused.

Getting a feel for how your presentation flows is

a great way to simmer down your content to the most potent ingredients.

Strategy Is Sacrifice

How much information can any person or group of people remember in a live moment?

I would argue, little. So, sacrifice all those points which aren't crucial. You can always collect them together and send them as a pre-read or a leave-behind after the presentation.

We need to determine what the important content is for your audience. What is the smallest amount of content possible, the sharpest, best content that adds to your pitch, your point, or your ask?

Great movies demonstrate the need for brevity. In a truly great film, every scene is crucial to the journey of the main characters and to the story that's been told.

The greatest film directors have the discipline to eradicate all those extraneous scenes. And instead, every scene moves the character forward, develops the narrative, advances the action, and delivers on the purpose of the film.

Similarly, in a pitch, every point, every slide has to move your story forward. And if it's not, if it's just there for interest's sake, you should remove it.

Subject matter experts believe that most of their content is important, right? And if you had more time or you were writing a book like this, maybe those digressions or nice-to-know pieces add to the texture. You can include them, but what we're talking about here is a pitch, a finely-tuned instrument that is laser-focused on one objective: to engage with your audience in a way where you and your content become unforgettable, something that moves them—something they say yes to.

So, if you think about the pitch or the public speaking moment in terms of the objective and get disciplined, you will start to remove the fat and end up with a highly powerful, much shorter presentation.

Let's go through the benefits.

Number one, highly memorable.

Number two, more manageable for you to rehearse and present.

Number three, your presentation gets past the croc brain into the rest of the human brain, so your content can be analysed and felt.

And four, it's easier for your audience to talk about afterwards. Often, we find ourselves pitching to people who are not the ultimate decision-makers. Therefore, we need our audience to take our ideas and push them up and around the organisation—and that's never going to happen if you've given someone a long-winded, bloated pitch that they can't pick up and work with.

Eight Minutes

This final tip is simple. Try to get your presentation down to eight minutes.

Often this means reducing your presentation by fifty-two minutes! Most meetings, and therefore presentations, are designed to be sixty minutes in length.

Even if you end up presenting it longer than eight minutes, just going through this exercise will help you identify the most critical points.

Interrogate every point and every slide. If it's not mission-critical, cut it. If it's not advancing your story, cut it. Anything that's included as broad context. Cut it.

As part of my role at Sohn Hearts & Minds, I work with the speakers to make their pitches compelling, attention-grabbing, and memorable, all within eight minutes. We focus on what we leave out more than what we include.

Getting serious about brevity is a strict and unforgiving process, but it will help you, and your audience, see the wood for the trees.

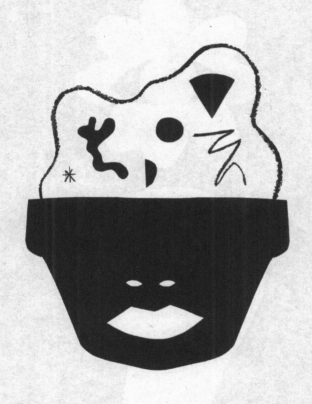

Conclusion

"Success is liking yourself,
liking what you do, and liking
how you do it."

—Maya Angelou

Talking about "winning" isn't something our culture encourages us to do. Everyone gets a participation award. But the truth is, you need to win every time you speak publicly. Win attention, win the esteem of your audience, win the decisions, win the money. I think the key is that everyone wins when it's done right. Creating a scenario that's a win-win is our ultimate goal. But the game is on, and winning has to be your objective. "Good enough" isn't it.

Thinking about presenting as a game shifts the objective of winning, and any stress around presenting, into a more playful territory. It's not about triumphing at someone else's expense: winning means we all benefit. But there's no getting away from the fact that you must perform at your best, aim for superb, and relish bringing the audience with you on the journey.

Extraordinary ideas are being dreamed up every day by people all over the world, but I know that most of those ideas won't happen. They won't become something concrete, become real, and have the impact they deserve to. If this book helps even one of those people to get their idea out of their head and into the world, I think I'll have done something worthwhile.

When I began to write this book, I intended to make the process, the techniques, and tips I've developed over the past twenty years easily accessible to anyone interested in becoming a better public speaker.

These aren't skills we learn at school or focus on developing in our careers. Even now, you could scrape through school without getting to be any good at presenting. This book aims to take what I've learned and make it accessible to anyone, anywhere. All you need is this book and some grit.

But for this book to make a difference for you, you're going to have to put in the hours. Do the work. Practice. Rehearse. Be accountable to yourself. Rehearse some more. Something I've learned in the ad game is how to commit: no hesitation, no negotiating with yourself. How to stop making excuses and just do it.

As I write, the pace of change continues to accelerate. Robots, AI, and whatever comes next will transform the world without question, but I'm certain that being live, telling stories, and having moments of inspiration that can change people's lives for the better is something uniquely human. That's the stuff that can't be replicated.

The best way to future-proof yourself is to get good at relationships and hone your emotional intelligence and ability to bring other people with you on a journey to somewhere new and different.

It's easy to talk about the concepts I've outlined but challenging to achieve on a meaningful level. But you can get there! And it doesn't involve a time-consuming retreat drinking only kombucha. It does take time, however, and it takes work.

If we think about all the biases, misunderstandings, errors in cognition, assumptions, and mixed messages brain science teaches us are taking place for most of us, most of the time, it's pretty close to miraculous that any of us get an idea across the line. We should think of the opportunity to try as bordering on a miracle too. Rare, precious, and unrepeatable moments that we would be crazy to squander. Preparing, rehearsing, and doing your best is critical if we want to win.

I've been lucky in my life. I get to do what I love every day, and I hope this book will help you do that too. I can't train everyone to be a brilliant public speaker, but I can share what I know. And maybe, when you're done with this book, you can give it to someone else who needs a boost to tell their unique story or suggest their brilliant solution to a problem.

I set the moral at the start: the ideas we can have as individuals are incredible, but to achieve truly great things, we need the belief and effort of other people.

I hope you now have everything you need to connect, collaborate, and use the collective's power to make a difference.

Now, you've just got to go and do it. I can't wait to hear how it goes.

About the Author

Jonathan Pease (JP) is a highly respected creative and communications expert with over twenty-five years of experience in the marketing and media industries.

JP started his career at the well-known advertising agency BBDO New York, where he learned the transformative power of great ideas and impactful pitching. Returning to Australia in 2003, JP founded the renowned ideas agency Tongue, which later became the Asia Pacific branch of the global agency AKQA. Today, he leads Delorean, a consultancy firm, and serves as Chief Creative Officer at We Are Unity, advising and investing in the success of clients such as agencies, multinationals, and start-ups. He also writes and directs feature films, ads, and other content and was awarded Best Director for his film *Two Bites* at the Sanctuary Cove International Film Festival in 2018.

A philanthropist, JP is a founding member of Australia's leading investment conference, Sohn Hearts & Minds, which has donated over fifty million dollars to medical research and and established an associated five hundred million dollar investment fund, HM1. As part of this role, he works with the speakers on their pitches each year. Speakers include Ray Dalio, Cathie Wood, Bill Ackman, Charlie Munger, Dan Ariely, and Professor Scott Galloway.

During his career, JP has worked with some of the most influential global brands, including Nike, Disney, Coca-Cola, Chanel, and M&M Mars, and has spoken at events such as Vivid, Remix, and Mumbrella.

He received his master of business from Sydney University and his bachelor's degree in marketing from the University of Technology Sydney/AdSchool.

Winning the Room is JP's debut book.

He currently lives in Australia, dividing his time between Sydney and Byron Bay with his wife Maddison and their four children—Kingston, Ripley, Ocean, and Lumi.

Mango Publishing, established in 2014, publishes an eclectic list of books by diverse authors—both new and established voices—on topics ranging from business, personal growth, women's empowerment, LGBTQ studies, health, and spirituality to history, popular culture, time management, decluttering, lifestyle, mental wellness, aging, and sustainable living. We were named 2019 *and* 2020's #1 fastest growing independent publisher by *Publishers Weekly*. Our success is driven by our main goal, which is to publish high-quality books that will entertain readers as well as make a positive difference in their lives.

Our readers are our most important resource; we value your input, suggestions, and ideas. We'd love to hear from you—after all, we are publishing books for you!

Please stay in touch with us and follow us at:

Facebook: Mango Publishing
Twitter: @MangoPublishing
Instagram: @MangoPublishing
LinkedIn: Mango Publishing
Pinterest: Mango Publishing
Newsletter: mangopublishinggroup.com/newsletter

Join us on Mango's journey to reinvent publishing, one book at a time.

Printed in the USA
CPSIA information can be obtained
at www.ICGtesting.com
JSHW03225210923
48917JS00004B/4